THE
COACH

Creating Partnerships for a Competitive Edge

THE COACH

Creating Partnerships for a Competitive Edge

Steven J. Stowell, Ph.D.
Matt M. Starcevich, Ph.D.

Published by
Center for Management
and Organization Effectiveness
1998

9146 South 700 East
Sandy, Utah
84070
(801) 569-3444

www.cmoe.com

First Edition Copyright © 1987
Revised Edition Copyright © 1998
The Center for Management
and Organization Effectiveness
9146 South 700 East
Sandy, Utah 84070

Steven J. Stowell, Ph.D.
Matt M. Starcevich, Ph.D.

ISBN: 0-9724627-2-4

Acknowledgement

We would like to express our deep appreciation for the support of those who encouraged, inspired, and assisted us over the last ten years, as this book became a reality.

Dr. Oakley Gordon and Linda Cruse were responsible for creating opportunities that made the research and data gathering possible. Deb Hedgepeth, Debbie Stowell, Helen Hodgson, and Debbie Gavellas played central roles in fine tuning, producing, and editing the manuscript. They were patient with our imperfections and worked hard to meet the deadlines.

Roy Yamahiro and Peter Block provided support and conceptual inspiration that has helped shape and influence our thinking about leadership in a positive and constructive way. We extend additional thanks to all of those in the client organizations that we have worked with to train managers in the coaching skills. Their confidence, feedback, and patience in staying with us during the years of refinement and improvement on the coaching model have been deeply appreciated. We hope these clients and future clients will enjoy the direction and depth of this material.

Lastly to Debbie Stowell, Judy Starcevich, and our families – their constant support and assistance have made our efforts enjoyable.

CMOE presents
the first in a series on

Partnerships in
the Work Place

**THE CENTER FOR MANAGEMENT AND
ORGANIZATION EFFECTIVENESS (CMOE)**

Organized in 1979 with the following mission:

- *To provide training for managers
  and employees*

- *To solve difficult organization problems*

- *To design and implement quality
  human resource systems*

- *To conduct practical and useful
  organizational research*

- *To publish the results of our work*

*Our staff all hold advanced degrees in the
behavioral sciences and consult with many of
the Fortune 500 firms to improve management
and organization effectiveness.*

Table of Contents

List of Illustrations

1

About This Book

WHY A REVISED EDITION

Classical paintings need touch up, hotels modernized, equipment overhauled, facilities freshened, and even garages cleaned and reorganized. Our motives with this revision were two fold. First to modernize the visual format of the material and secondly, to add 5 chapters to address repeated questions or concerns from participants in our workshops: The Five Levels of Coaching, Coaching Lessons From the World of Sports, Coaching at the Executive Level, Versatile Coaching and the Myers-Briggs Type Indicator, and Finding a Coach. The original skills and behaviors employed by effective coaches have stood the test of time and remain unchanged. The additions are enhancements and represent our efforts to continually improve the value added to our readers.

OUR PROMISE: WHY YOU SHOULD READ THIS BOOK

The role of the leader will be different in the future, different because of technological advances, increased competition (both domestic and international), and the desire of employees to be more involved in managing their own work. Leaders will need to instill a new competitive spirit in employees to streamline work, reduce errors, respond to customer needs, and solve challenging problems. People will have the greatest influence on productivity, excellence, and quality, but only if leaders can empower employees and give them more autonomy while maintaining effective accountability. This will mean a substantial change in the role of the traditional leader and in his/her skills to interact on a one-to-one basis. The new job of the leader will be to coach,

*New Age of
Leadership*

To Coach

develop, train, delegate, facilitate, and run interference rather than doing all the planning, organizing, and directing from an authoritative base.

In the future, leaders will be dealing with a more educated, talented group of employees who have definite interests and aspirations. Leaders and employees will become more like partners whose common cause will be to accomplish the job in the best way possible. Because organizations have defined resources and because actions that can be undertaken are limited, leaders and employees will need to develop a common vision of the mission or work to be done. Leaders will then coach, monitor, and help employees realize that vision and purpose. Leaders must learn how to convert employees into allies, not adversaries, without sacrificing standards of quality and productivity. In fact, the main reasons we advocate coaching are because it enables us to more adequately respond to the demands of customers, to maintain standards, and to fulfill the purpose of existing in the organization.

Some leaders may find this new approach to leadership challenging because their own leaders may not have been the best models to follow. In the past, we have looked at employees as children needing a benevolent parent rather than as entrepreneurial partners. More and more employees now want to be included, to contribute, and to be treated as necessary, not like just extra pairs of hands or pack mules. This new attitude will test the patience, skills, and knowledge of leaders.

So this book is about your beliefs as a leader regarding your employees and how they should be managed and directed in a very positive way. Our promise to you is that if you will seriously ponder the message of this book, begin practicing the behaviors, and assimilate the values advocated, you will succeed in winning the cooperation and support of your employees. It won't come overnight, and you will find some employees who defy the recommendations that we suggest. These exceptions will require a different and perhaps traditional management style. However, others will appreciate the refreshing difference in your approach and will reward you with incomparable levels of performance. We also promise to try to make the reading and search for solutions interesting and to the point.

So there you have it. There are many books on leadership. Choose this book if you want to concentrate on specific skills related to positive leadership and coaching interaction. We believe coaching is a constructive game for leaders to learn. A lot of games can be learned, some good, some not. Why not learn the art of a good one?

If you want specific leadership skills

GUIDE TO THIS BOOK

Not everyone likes to read a book from cover to cover. For those who like to pick and choose, here is a brief guide.

Chapter One, About This Book, is a summary of what we are advocating for future leader-employee relationships. Coaching plays a central role in creating and maintaining partner-oriented relationships.

Chapter 1

Chapter Two, Memories Never Die, is an intriguing story about a manager faced with a challenging coaching opportunity. As the story unfolds, the manager encounters obstacles and then discovers the actions that are needed to be a successful coach.

Chapter 2

Chapter Three, The Eight-Step Model, is a summary discussion of behaviors that we have discovered from our study of effective coaches. This model represents a road map for holding a successful coaching meeting.

Chapter 3

Chapter Four, The Five Levels of Coaching, is about coaching intensity. Many coaching situations are light, easy and fun. However, others are challenging, serious, and painful. All five levels require a different approach and mind set. Read this chapter and learn how to "tweak" the Coaching Model to give you the best possible outcome for each situation.

Chapter 4

Chapter Five, Versatile Coaching, is about personalities and individual differences. How do you adjust your coaching approach to accommodate and assimilate the wonderful uniqueness in our personalities? The MBTI is used as an example of how to understand personalities and flex your coaching style.

Chapter 5

Chapter Six, Supporting Skills, presents the skills that make the Eight-Step Model a positive and collaborative experience for the leader and employee. This chapter contains specific hints for the manager to follow when using the Eight-Step Model.

Chapter 6

Chapter Seven, The Coach's Contribution, explores a range

Chapter 7

of potential problems the manager must plan for. The manager's response to these issues will determine how he/she will approach and orchestrate the coaching meeting

Chapter 8

Chapter Eight, Coaching Lessons from the World of Sports, is about the differences and similarities between these very different environments. There are good and bad lessons from the often over exposed romanticized world of sports.

Chapter 9

Chapter Nine, Positive Motivational Coaching, takes the Eight-Step Model beyond working with specific problems to coaching the above-average performer, or the employee who has no performance problem but needs a challenge or more job satisfaction in order to contribute to the organization.

Chapter 10

Chapter Ten, Finding a Coach, explores the criteria for selecting a coach and how to work out an understanding or agreement with someone who can fulfill the coaching role for you.

Chapter 11

Chapter Eleven, Coaching at the Executive Level, is about focusing the Coaching process on executive level relationships, performance issues, team leadership, and adapting to change. Many assume that those who rise to the top are excluded from coaching initiatives. This can be a disastrous assumption and one that is thoroughly explored in this chapter.

Chapter 12

Chapter Twelve, Concluding Thoughts, presents a number of ideas that help put the entire coaching process into perspective (Beyond Coaching, Group Problem Solving, etc.). Look at these as bonus ideas to help make what you have learned even more effective.

Appendix

In the *Appendix,* you will find a planning guide for the coaching session and a summary of the training design we have used to teach these concepts and skills to thousands of managers.

We hope this guide will help in making your reading more enjoyable and productive for you. Let's get started!

PARTNERSHIPS ARE EVERYWHERE

Leaders are partners first

You hear a lot about partnerships in life, in marriages, business, tennis, or bridge. There are investment partnerships, limited partnerships, law or CPA partnerships; in short, the term partnership is applied to many types of relationships. It usually creates positive visions and feelings within us, and coaching can be defined as a meaningful partnership with employees that includes these positive visions and feelings. We believe that the role of leaders and partners should be fused: great leaders must be partners first. Increasingly, workers are adopting the philosophy that the only relationship deserving of loyalty and allegiance is that which is freely granted by the employee.

Webster defines a partner as an ally or an association built around common interests and goals. The concept denotes cooperation in a joint venture or challenge. A partnership is a relationship that emphasizes equal status (rather than inequality) and encompasses a certain independence as well as certain obligations and commitments. Partnerships usually require direct interaction and contact. A good partnership is like a good contract: It requires mutual consent, valid consideration from both parties, and willingness to respond to the other's highest-level needs first.

Definition

We are strong advocates of partnerships because leaders and employees have more significant commonalties than differences:

- *Both have a lot to gain if the other succeeds.*
- *Both have careers and mortgages on the line if they fail.*
- *Both have to be concerned about the efficient use of resources.*
- *Both have to take risks in order to survive and prosper in challenging environments.*

In contrast, leader-employee differences tend to be minor:

- *The job titles are a little different.*
- *The leader's box on the organization chart is 1/4 inch higher on the page.*
- *The leader has a bigger paycheck and bigger mortgage.*
- *The leader gets chewed out first and the employee second if the unit fails on assignments.*

Partnerships are strengthened through positive motivational coaching as well as honest problem-solving coaching. Coaching is the most useful tool in building "master" partnerships with each employee on a one-to-one basis. In essence, partnerships are a way of achieving a mature, adult-

Coaching: a tool for building partnerships

to-adult relationship with employees.

Good coaching depends on good leaders, and leadership is a unique phenomenon in any organization. It is unique because the corporation can more easily control other elements of the business than it can the quality of leadership and partnerships. Leadership is elusive; it is mainly defined by who you are and what you want to make of it.

It's in your control

As a leader, you largely determine the quality of relationships despite any rules and policies of the company that encourage quality leadership. The fact of the matter is that poor leaders can hide behind "busy work" and activities. The decision is yours.

Organizations need leaders who are personally committed to the idea of building partnerships with employees. Sure, it's easier said than done, especially when others who have influence and occupy leadership positions above yours are not as concerned with building partnerships as you are. Usually, when we raise this topic with groups, everyone nods and says, "Right on." The only problem is we never seem to be working with the group who needs to develop these skills. We are told that we need to work with higher management or lower management, or the personnel people, but each of those groups recommends some group other than themselves. When we work with these other groups, they say the same thing. . . so far we haven't been able to find the right group.

The reality for most organizations is that great leadership, at the working level, is still largely wishful thinking, often seen as a luxury that can't be afforded. Our position is that no one can afford to wait for good leadership in today's competitive environment. The problem is that when cash is tight, most firms are willing to "mortgage their future" and save a few dollars by cutting their leadership development efforts, throwing espoused leadership principles out the window and reverting to "tough tactics" with employees. And many individual managers know that as long as they keep their heads down and look busy, no one will bug them about stuff like "partnerships." Furthermore, a good working manager usually has a hard time breaking away from the press of the daily routine. We believe this "activity trap" is literally addictive and keeps leaders away from partnership building. Daily demands push leaders into doing things right (details) rather than into doing the right things (concentrating on really important tasks).

Let's face it. A lot of worthy activities that need to get done fly in the face of making leadership and people number one in the corporation. Our best assessment is that in most organizations people are number seven on the priority list and moving up slowly.

Somehow leaders have to learn to be more effective at balancing and shifting from activities to serious leadership.

As much value needs to be put on excellence in leadership as on excellence in managing activities (like having a clean desk, filling out time cards, and checking reports). We have to get away from the notion that to further your career ambitions, you need only manage activities well. Leaders need to concentrate more on effective leadership right where they are and not worry about trying to look good on the surface for the sake of a little upward mobility.

It's leadership , not activity

The task of the "leader-partner" is to establish goals and missions, to listen, to be accessible and understanding, to empower others, and to maintain accountability. Leaders need foresight and must build their organization into a productive community. They need to have a sense of unlimited liability for their employees' productivity and development and to display unconditional support and concern.

The task

Our contention and central point is that leader-employee partnerships are in trouble. Actually, if you take an objective look at the situation, leader-employee partnerships have never been out of trouble in American industry because the power and benefits of really strong, meaningful leader-employee partnerships in the workplace have never been duly recognized. Traditionally, leaders and employees have acted more like adversaries than like partners. Relationships in the past have been marked by caution, some secretiveness, high authority, and heavy control.

We've never had it!!

The goal of the coaching process is to create durable partnerships that can easily withstand the stress and agonies of problem solving and enjoy the joys and benefits of positive and motivational coaching. Accepting an employee as a partner means the leader respects his/her stewardship, honors the rights of the employee, and in a business sense, uses the human resource effectively by taking full advantage of its wisdom, skills, and potential. A leader becomes not a critic but rather a coach and helper. Often, leaders want to coach an employee but come off sounding like a critic who just wasted an evening at the opening of a mediocre Broadway musical. In either situation, the reviews are particularly painful for those involved. They tear people down and affect their self-esteem. The leader as a coach must try hard to avoid this type of confrontation. The way a leader views employees, or the status of the employees in the mind of the leader, will probably be reflected in the way they are treated in a coaching discussion.

What form of partnership do you want? Concentrating on leadership means that you need to make some very clear conscious choices about the types or forms of partnerships you want to create with your employees. Like it or not, either productive or counterproductive partnerships will emerge. Our feeling is that leaders can take an active role in shaping and building the kind of partnerships they want. The choice boils down to a selection from four basic types: adversarial, patriarchal, silent, or entrepreneurial.

1-Adversarial The first type of partnership is steeped in American history, and particularly in the history of the industrial revolution. It is also the partnership model used by the military (quite successfully in some situations). We believe this "adversarial model of partnerships" motivates workers to seek the help of unions and third-party representation. Historically, leaders of profit-motivated organizations harbored these assumptions about their employee partners: "Employees are lazy, greedy, and stupid. Consequently we will pay them only for the work they do, we won't trust them with responsibility, we will design their jobs so simply that monkeys could handle them, and we will keep tight control on them." People were viewed as just another resource, like equipment and buildings; they were taught not to think but simply to submit to authority. What does this approach do to the attitude of employee partners? They resent it and are bored by their work. They become cautious and overly dependent on leaders for every instruction. Because they are not empowered to do anything on their own, they feel confined and relate the organization to a penal institution. Leaders are perceived as bosses and bullies. We even have a hard time suggesting that this is a form of partnership. But it exists today, too frequently in fact. This approach has been hard to eliminate because in an earlier time it worked. It helped make America great, and so a lot of people who are resistant to change have adopted an attitude of "Why knock it?"

The next type of partnership is born out of family and parental experiences, the "patriarchal partnership." Here the leader plays the role of father or mother. It is different from an adversarial partnership in that the leader-parent or patriarch means well, wants the best for the employee-child, and wants to provide protection. The relationship is seductive and feels good. In this partnership, the employees assumes that if they keep their heads down and don't ask a lot of questions, they will get ahead and things will work out. This partnership causes employees to feel and act like children. *2-Patriarch/ Matriarch*

Risk taking is not encouraged. The employees can take comfort in the fact that nothing will ever be their fault. Everything can always be blamed on the leader. Approval is sought from Dad or Mom. This partnership rests on accountability and control, but includes very little autonomy to stretch, to be innovative, or to grow in abilities and talent. Employees are robbed of their aspirations, dreams, and self-confidence.

The next type of partnership is the "silent partnership," which is far too common in industry today. The silent partnership is born out of leader apathy and benign neglect. We see a lot of working managers who are willing to accept whatever level of performance they happen to get from their employees. Sometimes these working managers just don't appear to notice or observe what is really going on in their organization. At times, they seem inattentive and even uninterested in employee behavior and good leadership. Other silent leaders more consciously abdicate their leadership responsibilities because they don't really like leadership tasks and get more satisfaction from being busy doing their own thing. Whether the apathy and silence are intentional or not, the result is the same: employees feel unchallenged, neglected, and unappreciated. They don't grow and learn from the leader's experience and knowledge. This style of partnership is a mixed blessing. The good news is employees have a lot of autonomy, and that's great if all of the employees are talented self-starters. In fact, being a leader would be simple if employees were perfect. However, the imperfec- *3-Silent* tions in employees give the job of leader its meaning. The bad news about the silent leader is the lack of control and accountability. Silent partnerships do not work because whatever success the unit achieves will result from the behavior of those who work for the silent leader. An effective leader can't be passive and content but must be an active force for setting the direction and improving and shaping the efforts of the employees.

4-Entrepreneurial   The fourth type of partnership, born out of the need to have a strong competitive unit, is what we call the "entrepreneurial partnership." The leader in this partnership maintains high accountability and high autonomy. The partnership requires serious collaboration and coaching from the leader. Regular interactions have purpose and meaning. Problems are confronted in a supportive fashion, and successes are acknowledged and reinforced. The leader-employee pair work and collaborate in an effort to do whatever is necessary to see that each other's performance is maximized and that the unit functions efficiently. It is no different from any other type of successful partnership in life. However, the organizational hierarchy and the risk of learning to trust others, unfortunately, force some distortion in potentially good partnerships. An entrepreneurial partnership feels different; it creates doubts and goes against the traditional grain of organizations. At first, it feels a little bit intimidating to work with employees who are empowered as partners. Moving to the more ideal entrepreneurial partnership means that you are choosing:

It means
- *to be an architect of your unit vs. another laborer or expert*
- *to be a resource/helper vs. an obstacle/constraint*
- *to be open with information*
- *to value accountability and results vs. control and rules*
- *to value autonomy and risk taking vs. dependency and cautiousness*
- *to see the unit become competitive and great vs. achieving personal fame and visibility*
- *to be direct and authentic with employees vs. indirect and manipulative*
- *to be a coach and problem solver vs. a criticizer and complainer*

These statements represent the vision of the entrepreneurial partnership. The way to move closer to achieving the entrepreneurial partnership is through regular contact and coaching. Coaching is the key mechanism for partnership building and maintenance. It gives you the opportunity to change and focus behavior that you consider unacceptable, or to motivate and reinforce behavior that you find desirable. Each coaching session is the ultimate stage for acting out the type of partnership that you want to create.

Through regular contact and coaching

The partner-oriented mentality views employees as equals with a lot at stake in the workplace. Employees who are able and want to contribute and those who are close to and familiar with the work should have the opportunity. Employees who can't currently contribute to the partnership or to the resolution of job challenges and problems need to be brought along more slowly. If they choose not to participate, you need to say goodbye to them compassionately and gracefully.

Not all employees want, nor do they deserve, partnership status. Some employees treat the leader and the job as impersonally as some leaders treat employees. However, we believe that the leader is responsible for initiating a change in the nature of the relationship and communicating the concepts of partnership to the employees. It is a key leadership responsibility to coach, train, and develop employees, and this is one major distinguishing feature of the leader's role as compared to the employee's.

Through ten years of research and observation, we have found that skillful leaders rely less on authority and dictums and more on collaboration and negotiation. Effective leaders use their ability to reason, to ask penetrating questions, and to listen, rather than relying on the official authority of their position. Finally, we have noticed that effective leaders can blend and weave ideas and solutions, and that they defer to the employee when appropriate. If you push, hammer, and require employees who are potential partners and allies to work in a bent-over position, they naturally become angry and withdraw their valuable support and cooperation. Although they will perform according to your wishes as long as you are watching closely, you will have created conflict and resentment that will have a nasty and lasting emotional effect. The result is usually an erosion of trust which requires

What effective leaders do

"Great leaders try to understand before they expect to be understood."

time and a lot of good-faith actions to restore. If you push people around and act like "king of the hill," employees will respond by acting and thinking like gofers.

The key is teamwork

In developing a partnership with your employees, you are aiding them in achieving their potential. The key to success is teamwork. The better one partner looks, the better the other one will too. The fundamental goal and underlying premise of any coaching discussion or intervention is always mutual benefit.

Entrepreneurial partnership: That's what this book is all about.

A lot of power and creativity can come from building and maintaining a good partnership. Those of us who have been in one can vouch for this from first-hand experience. Partnerships don't always guarantee that times will be easy, but they do mean the difficult times and problems can be overcome and solved. A lot of candor, skill, and courage are required to talk straight to your partner (be they employee, spouse, or investor). Leaders must find space in their busy days to create positive partnerships with their employees. That's what this book is all about. We hope you will enjoy reading about the coaching process and how it can be the key to creating an "entrepreneurial" partnership.

2

Memories Never Die

"You're not going to like what I've got to say, and I don't want you to blame me for this, but management feels it's best for you to speak to Pat directly. Since she'll be returning to your department, you can make the chain of command clear to her from the beginning." Fred's news totally ruined my day. I swallowed my resentment but couldn't help thinking, "Why can't you talk to her? I didn't make the decision to put her back into my department." The whole fiasco was an incredible turn of events.

I can still look back and remember Pat's first day on the job after I hired her two years ago. She was determined to do well, was eager to please, and appeared to want to get ahead. But most of all, I was struck by her attractiveness and irresistible social skills. As time passed, it became increasingly obvious that her presence in my department was a mixed blessing. I couldn't help liking her. She was bright and learned fast, maybe too fast. Family problems had forced her to drop out of college after completing three years towards a Bachelor's degree in business, but she had immediately enrolled in night school and was well on her way to finishing her degree. At 28, Pat showed occasional signs of brilliance and the potential to mature into a highly valued employee. When I had needed her help most, she came through with creative solutions to problems and willingly worked overtime to see them become reality.

I felt that she had the ability to go a long way in this organization, so it bothered me when I began to see the limitations. Rumors began to circulate about her, minimal at first, that she would use any means available to advance her career. In important subtle ways, she wasn't fitting into the culture of the organization. Intimate personal relationships

Pat's past

with co-workers might be okay in other organizations but not in this archaic institution.

I felt that I was on the firing line. She had so many strengths, but my instincts warned me that she was cunning and deceptive, perhaps willing to put her own needs above the best interests of the company. I became increasingly torn about her value as an employee and finally called her in to discuss my concern.

"Pat, I want you to know first that I value your work and I have no desire to limit your personal freedoms, but please don't let your personal objectives interfere with the ability of other employees to do their jobs. And the same holds true with our customers; they can't be compromised." I'll never forget the look of deep and genuine hurt that Pat couldn't hide, but her response was professional.

"I had no idea that you were thinking those things about me. I'm glad you spoke to me. I'll really pay more attention to what I'm doing. I don't want to be misunderstood. You've got to know that I want what is best for the company as well as for my own career."

She sounded so sincere that day we talked; it was no wonder that I was disappointed when her actions seemed to belie her words.

And along comes Bob

I have to admit that Pat wasn't the only one swept off her feet by Bob. He was appointed the new Director of Sales and Marketing about six months after Pat began working with my department. Bob was a highly capable individual, and I admired him as well. He had the rare combination of hard-driving intensity coupled with a deep concern for people. Customers were a high priority for him. He'd push the staff to work long hours to have projects completed on time. He wasn't always popular in that regard. He always maintained personal contact with customers, as well as staff, from the beginning to the end of even the smallest job. It was no wonder that he was known for his ability to create new markets for the company's services. On the other hand, some people saw Bob as using his personality and charisma to pull him through on big deals and, I must admit that he struck me as something of the flamboyant, high-roller type.

It made sense that Bob liked working with Pat. Whenever projects involved both our departments, they'd come back from lunch brimming with energy, new ideas, and plans when most of the staff was content to relax after too satisfying a lunch. It was their combined energy that propelled the office on the big and more difficult projects.

That was when the rumors intensified. At first they seemed petty – the references to long lunches or weekends spent in the office together working on projects – but I began to notice things too. The casual lunches developed into lengthier ones and soon an afternoon off now and then. That was when I became alarmed and decided to talk to her again. I could see the effects on the morale of the team.

What's going on?

"Pat, look. . . you're an adult, I can't tell you what to do with your personal life. But I am concerned about the level of teamwork and the reputation our entire department is getting. I don't want you to get hurt in this situation. I've seen too many people end up holding the bag." I must admit that I found it painfully difficult to confront an employee who was basically good and had a lot of potential. My feelings reminded me of a favorite quotation mounted on my office wall:

> *"Coaching is the most uncomfortable, avoided, and mishandled of all management tasks."*

I guess things happened faster than even I had imagined. Pat's promotion was very much on the "Q.T." Her position wasn't even posted for people to bid on. In fact, the way I heard about it was a "post-it-note" on my door from Bob, the Marketing Director, informing me that Pat had been promoted to the position of Senior Client Sales Representative in his division. I couldn't have been happier. A nasty problem had been plucked off my back, and Bob and Pat were no longer my concern. By this time, rumors about their affair were out in the open, although they seemed to work harder and pretend that nothing was going on. It was no secret that Bob always closed the door when he had individual consultations with Pat. He never made that a practice with the other sales reps. I can tell you one thing for sure: Bob's boss wasn't about to confront him. After all, Bob was delivering exactly what he had been hired to deliver.

Pat's promotion

Bob had been working with the company for over a year when management intervened. It was all pretty hush-hush at first, until the facts gradually came to light about Bob and his manipulative style. Rumors were rampant about how Bob had overstepped his approval of authority on some major deals and then, to top it off, I think that management got a little tired of Bob's expense account. More and more, Bob wanted to play this game according to his rules, and I think top management was getting a little tired and felt

Bob's luck ends threatened by Bob's success. From that point on, the stories got a little weird. All anyone knew for certain was that Bob was in his office the next day, packing up his personal belongings. The official announcement from the CEO was curt: "Due to alternative career interests, the Director of Sales and Marketing has elected to pursue other career options, and his resignation has been regretfully accepted. I hope you will join with me in wishing Bob the best of luck in his new endeavors in the Yukon." Not a bad cover-up if the rumors hadn't circulated so quickly. As it turned out, the CEO would have been better off if he had just leveled with everyone about why Bob was fired.

Pat's demotion As far as I was concerned, it didn't make a lot of difference what happened to Bob and Pat. The bottom line was that now I had to handle the whole messy situation and at that point, it was hard for me to remember anything good about Pat. One thing was certain. She wouldn't take a demotion and pay cut lying down. I don't know which I dreaded worse: telling her or my department.

People were resentful when she was promoted so quickly. Her new job had been exciting, much more than the one that she left. It would be painful to come back to a job with so much less potential and prestige, not to mention the cut in pay and to work with people who talked about her behind her back.

Why me? As I drove home, I tried to sort through all my thoughts and feelings. Why is this such a problem for me? For the most part I am a pretty good manager. I try hard, and I have been with the organization eight years. I think most of my people would rate me as a good leader. I try to stay up on management articles, and I attend at least one workshop each year to be prepared for situations like this. Like most managers I am faced with a lot of time pressures and I feel caught in the middle of daily routines and activities. I probably spend too much time making sure everything is done right, the details, and not enough time on doing the things that matter more in the long run. I tell everyone that I have one of the best groups of employees that a manager could ask for. But I have to admit that, when it comes right down to it, I see things every day that could be done differently and more effectively.

Pat isn't the only one who could use a little more attention from me. Frankly, if I had my choice, I would much rather do other things than confront employees about things that need attention or improvement. Besides, I don't think they gave me this manager's job because of my proven leadership skills. I was promoted because I was a damn good technician, because I got my monthly reports in on time, and because I completed my projects under budget. Even when I try to put in ten-hour days, it still seems like my leadership responsibilities suffer. You know, maybe that's why I am putting in ten-hour days; maybe I am doing a lot of work that belongs to others and there isn't enough teamwork in the department. With any other group of employees, I would probably be putting in seven or eight-hour days. . . . But why does it seem like it's always me who gets to handle miserable situations like the one with Pat?

I had little appetite for dinner and could tell it was going to be one of those nights. I finally retreated to my den and reached for my journal to make my routine daily entries. This journal has preserved much of what I have learned in trying to help Pat weather a major crisis in her professional life. In hopes that these concepts might also be of use to you, the reader, the relevant entries accompany my story.

MY JOURNAL

As I picked up the pencil and my grip tightened, I could feel the tenseness. I had a hard time recalling anything about my day except the anger and resentment caused by the predicament with Pat. I wanted to remind her about all her mistakes, what they were costing, and how they had put her career in a hole. For some reason I had backed off these negative emotions, maybe because I had put myself into her shoes.

Negative emotions create negative actions and reactions.

As I reflected on situations with other employees, I could envision how a positive mindset had helped me and how painfully long it had taken me before I realized it. Like it or not, my attitude would play just as important a role in the resolution of this issue. I started to think about why and how Pat had gotten into a mess so contrary to my wishes and the culture of the organization. The more I tried to make sense out of this, the less I could. I asked myself whether it was important to understand why, or whether I should accept the situation as a fait accompli. What I realized was that Pat needed a manager who wouldn't exacerbate her painful rejection.

I don't have to understand why in order to be helpful.

That realization helped to minimize the confusion I felt. I began to focus more on the end result I wanted from this situation. I didn't want to get aggressive with Pat, yet it seemed like a disservice to withhold information. Could she be expected to change if she didn't have a clear picture of the situation? I felt torn; I wanted to be nice as well as honest. The manager I admired most in life had that very impressive ability.

People appreciate an honest confrontation as long as they don't feel pushed in the process.

Having worked through my approach, I was beginning to feel better. This felt like the type of role I wanted to play. I went to bed thinking that I had the situation under control. I would meet with Pat the next day, break the news to her, and then wait a week for things to settle down before I met with her again. There was no doubt in my mind that we would have lots to talk about after a week back in my department. I slipped my pocket calendar from my briefcase and made a commitment: a second meeting with Pat at 11:30 a.m., a week from the initial meeting.

Friday, March 26

My carefully reasoned analysis of the situation and my optimism about facing Pat had vanished by the next morning. I awoke with a clear sense of impending doom and was praying for a miracle. But when neither the Good Witch of the North nor the Blue Fairy appeared, I resigned myself to the meeting.

First discussion with Pat

Once I accepted the inevitable, I decided that I might as well get it over with. I headed for Pat's office as soon as I arrived at work. One look at her and I knew that bringing her back into the department was not going to be easy. She greeted me with a mixture of relief and hostility. I didn't waste any time, "Pat, I'm sure you've been wondering how you would be affected now that Bob has left the company. I don't know if you'll like this a whole lot, but management has decided to reassign you to your old job in my department."

Pat went white. It was clear that this was not what she had been expecting. "I don't believe it. That's not fair! I'm being discriminated against! That's insane. I'll file a complaint."

Her anger was so apparent that I felt myself getting defensive and wanting to argue back. Knowing that wouldn't help, I asked her to consider the situation more realistically. "Weren't you using Bob for your own ends, just as he was using you?"

"So you believe the rumors too! I work hard at my job. I was promoted because of the work I've done and my abilities, not my relationship with Bob. Now what will people be saying? How in the world do you expect me to face the people in that department?"

"Fireworks"

When she had calmed down a little, I explained how we would bring her back into the department and what my expectations were. I reminded her of the problems that I had noticed before she was promoted and made it clear that certain standards would have to be met.

Despite Pat's anger, disappointment, and now unnerving silence, I tried to convince myself that she would cooperate. What other choice did she have? She'd pulled through before. I left her office with a cautious optimism that things would work out. There was even a sense of relief. . . giving her the bad news was behind me.

The next few days revealed that any optimism was premature. The effect that Pat was having on the department was decidedly negative. She was resentful and defensive, and people were rapidly getting tired of it. To make matters worse, she seemed to be intentionally sabotaging the work of the department in an effort to get even. People were becoming increasingly angry, and I feared open revolt. It made me question my leadership skills. Why was I letting this situation get out of control? Did Pat really have a potential that was worth trying to protect and foster? What could I do or say that would let her know I understood how angry and hurt she was and, at the same time, motivate her to see her experience with Bob as something she had learned from and moved beyond?

Pat's performance deteriorates.

Pat was losing what little respect of her colleagues she had left. Few of them had seen her tremendous creativity, her ability to produce under pressure. I often wished that I hadn't either. Firing her would be painful, but, on the plus side, termination would be a quick and permanent solution. Instead, I was torn between that alternative and trying to salvage the situation. Maybe I wasn't capable of turning this around, but then this would be my failure as well as hers. I wasn't quite ready to admit defeat.

Monday, April 5

I had put a busy week behind me, the problem with Pat pushed out of mind by immediate office demands. Monday started out wonderfully! I woke up early, had time for a leisurely jog, and even spent twenty minutes in my den reviewing files and preparing for a luncheon meeting with my boss and some new managers. As I do every morning, I checked my calendar book. Suddenly, what was written there seemed to reach out and choke me. No matter how I tried, I couldn't deny that I had written the words, "11:30 A.M. consultation with Pat." I really didn't need this. Why did it have to be today? I wildly considered alternatives, but none of them worked. My mind was reeling with anxiety. I was trying to think fast. There must be some way to escape from another confrontation with Pat. Then I stopped, as I realized my motives. "What am I doing? Am I running away from this?"

Constructive openness with employees takes a lot of leadership courage!

I remember reading that employees are more willing to get feedback than leaders are willing to give it. I recommitted to myself that I would not fall into the avoidance trap or take the easy way out. Besides, I knew my boss would call me before 12:00 for the luncheon meeting we had with the new managers. I figured I could "gut" it out for 20 or 30 minutes, and then I would be rescued.

Mornings pass quickly when the worst is ahead. It seemed like 11:30 was there in a lightening flash. I hesitated as I picked up the phone and reluctantly dialed Pat's extension. I don't think I have ever talked that fast in my life, but she managed to understand that I was asking her to take a break from her work and join me in my office for a minute.

Second discussion with Pat

The atmosphere was icy when she walked in and sat down. I was nervous. Whatever little confidence I'd had drained away, leaving an empty feeling in the pit of my stomach. I searched for words, "Can I get you something?" It sounded like I was stalling for time. I closed the door to my office. The sound echoed like a vault closing shut. My leg hit the corner of a magazine rack as I headed to safety behind my desk.

She sat down. It was hard to make eye contact. The silence was deafening. I had to say something. "Uh. . . Pat, do you know why I called you in?" She didn't say anything. That didn't feel like much of a start, but I assumed that she was giving me the green light. "Pat I'm going to get right to the point. I think you have a real attitude problem." Pat rigidly sat up in her chair. She seemed to bristle at this comment. I barged ahead before she could say anything, pointing out that sometimes the truth is painful.

Pat interrupted me and said, "It is not fair. . . it's just not fair." She was getting highly emotional, and I could see that my words had cut pretty deep. I knew I would have to pick up the momentum if we were to make any progress.

Emotions rise

"Sometimes life isn't fair. Look, Pat, you have a choice. You can grow up and learn something from this, or you can just run away."

Pat tried to cut in on me. "It's not my fault," she shouted. "It's theirs."

My voice grew stronger. "I don't want to hear about your excuses. I just want to be honest with you, and I want you to be honest with yourself."

"You've got it all wrong. You have no idea what's been going on. I'm perfectly capable of doing my job. Where do you get off on this anyway? Don't you think it's time for you to stop attacking me? You tell me I can turn over a new leaf, and then you don't give me a chance. I'm sick of it, all of it."

"Stop attacking me."

"Look, Pat, the facts are the facts. You need to quit pouting and take more interest in your work. Everyone in the department has mentioned to me that you're cutting yourself off from the rest of them, and that's creating a communication breakdown that I can't live with!"

Pat responded quickly, "What do you think? Is that how you've seen me acting?"

The silence was deafening.

"Who do you believe? Me or them?"

"Look," I told her, "all I want you to do is stay in the department and try. But if things don't change, I'll guarantee you it will cost you on your next performance appraisal and on your salary adjustment. I think it's only fair to the rest of the department. Unless you shape up, I'll be forced to explore with management the possibility of a transfer into another group where teamwork isn't so critical."

At that, Pat exploded. "If you don't like my work, then get rid of me. If communication is what you want, I can handle it, but people in the department better quit treating me like some carnival side show. They better get off my back."

Saved by the bell

At that moment the phone rang. . . it was my boss saying he was ready for the meeting. I put down the receiver and stood up, "Look, Pat, I didn't want to cut this short, but maybe we shouldn't push this further today. We both need to think about it more before we talk again." It suddenly seemed to be totally out of control, and I pleaded with Pat, "We have to make this thing work. Everyone is watching. Just remember, I hired you. My credibility is on the line too."

Pat just stared at me as if she couldn't believe what she was hearing. "Look, I was promoted because I can handle a challenging job. Just tell me what you want, and leave my personal life and personal choices out of it! They're not your concern. Can't you understand that. . ."

"Look, Pat," I interrupted, "let's not blow this out of proportion. I want you to figure out a way to turn this around. . . okay?" By this time I was cramming files into my briefcase like clothes into a suitcase when I was late for a plane. I headed for the door brushing past her as she stood up and started to say something. But I was out the door and walking fast when my thoughts caught up with me.

"Wow, that was close, 20 minutes of pure hell, and it felt like an hour." A little of the tension subsided as I crossed the parking lot. I hated to admit it, but I was relieved when the phone rang. I felt that I was getting nowhere; Pat just didn't believe me or see that she needed to change her behavior and improve the situation. I wished that there was a way to put up a mirror so that she could see what the rest of the department had been seeing for the past week.

Where did I go wrong?

As I thought back over the way I had handled myself at that meeting, I flinched at my own inability to confront her. How could she have discussed or been honest about anything the way I never stopped talking. . . and what was it that she had been about to say as I brushed by her at the door?

As I joined the others for lunch, I couldn't keep my mind off Pat. If she was responsible for the breakdown in our communication, why was I feeling so bad? Our meeting just hadn't gone the way I had intended.

Lunch with my boss

When my boss asked me to provide some very specific information about how my department could help solve a problem, it was hard to break out of my thoughts. I became confused and had trouble keeping the thread of the discussion. In my fumbling attempt to both disguise and explain my confusion, I began to tell him about the problems with Pat. He was quiet – that confident, unemotional exterior of his emphasizing my agitation. He took off his glasses and methodically rubbed the bridge of his nose. Then he spoke. "We've talked about this type of situation before. You know what top management wants – a smoothly run ship. I can count on you to handle this, can't I?"

"Thanks a lot"

I was fumbling again. "Well, sure, boss, no problem. You can count on me to straighten Pat out."

"I'm counting on you to keep this from becoming an embarrassment." He put his glasses back on, sat back in his chair, and looked at me. "And now we've got some more important issues to cover."

That was definitely the end of that conversation. Great! A little more pressure, just what I needed when I couldn't see my way out of this mess. I sure didn't get any help from my boss on how to best handle Pat.

More pressure

I returned to the office after lunch, dreading the thought that I might run into Pat. I wanted to think through our meeting, but any further exchange with her was not likely to help. I needn't have worried. A note from her was sitting on my desk. "My doctor was able to give me an appointment. I will be gone until morning." What kind of a manager was I? My confidence in my ability to solve this problem was eroding further as I realized that Pat was at least as upset as I was.

Where to turn? I felt as if I was rolling down a mountainside with no one to break my fall. Wallowing in self-pity didn't seem like a long-term solution, so I racked my brain for someone who could help. I decided to call Judy, our Personnel Representative, who has exceptional people skills and had helped me out of some tough personnel problems in the past. I guess the tension must have been obvious in my voice, as she interrupted me, "Let me come over. I can

Maybe Judy can help.

tell this is bothering you. See you in five minutes." Just taking that first step toward solving the problem gave me a glimmer of hope.

How did you prepare for the meeting?

"Okay," said Judy, "so you had a difficult discussion with Pat. Let's go back and look at the way you got ready for that meeting."

"Do you think that's really necessary? I mean I've got a problem facing me right now!"

"Maybe not," she said, "but I'd like to have the full picture, so review with me what you did."

"Well, last week was a busy one; when I realized that I'd scheduled a meeting with Pat for today, I just went ahead and kept our appointment."

"Let me try this one," Judy said. "You're a very conscientious manager, so tell me how you spend your time before a budget review with top management?"

"Great," I thought, "I need some specific advice about a critical personnel issue, and she's going to analyze my budget review process." Just before I gave her a smart remark, I realized what she was driving at. I spent a lot of time understanding every detail, rationale, and possible alternative behind the budget my staff puts together.

"You're smiling. What's funny?" she asked.

"I am smiling, but only at what I was just thinking. It's really not funny that I spend a lot of time preparing for my budget meeting and spent very little time actually preparing for my meeting with Pat. I have been worrying about Pat, but I haven't been doing any real planning."

"I thought you'd see the point."

I could sense that Judy's insights would be of long-term value for me so I took out a pencil and pad to reserve the key ideas from our discussion for my journal. I titled it PREPARATION.

Preparation

Do your homework: gather objective data don't rely on assumptions or hearsay evidence.

Just as it was to Judy, my lack of preparation had been obvious to Pat. I started to squirm as I replayed a part of our conversation: "Everyone in the department has mentioned to me that you're cutting yourself off from the rest of them, and that's creating a communication barrier." I sounded like a manager, strong and informed, but when Pat had pressed me, I was forced to admit that I couldn't support what I was saying. My observations were vague, and I didn't have the facts.

Judy broke into my thoughts, "It's important to think positively as we talk and not get bogged down worrying about what has already happened. How much time can we spend on this?"

"As much time as we need. This is very important to me, and I. . ."

"What's the matter?" she asked.

I couldn't believe my own ears. I was willing to spend more time talking about this with Judy than I was willing to commit to Pat. But hadn't my boss given me a book called The One Minute Administrator?

Judy laughed when I mentioned this. "I think you know the difference between a leader and an administrator? It's just a matter of time."

"Tell me some words that would capture what you were thinking right before the meeting with Pat." She caught me off guard, so I just blurted out my immediate thoughts: "Well I wanted to get it over with. I felt nervous and uncomfortable; I sure as heck didn't want to give in to Pat. I knew it wouldn't be any fun and that we would end up arguing with each other."

One minute won't cut it. Allow at least 30-40 minutes.

"So when you think about it, you had a negative picture of how the meeting would go from the beginning."

She was right. I had set myself up for failure. Everything I had thought about was negative. I hadn't gone over the positive things I wanted to do and say. . . my focus had been on defensive tactics and that alone. If all I thought about before a meeting was what could go wrong and how negative it would be, sure enough those things would happen.

Judy just nodded her approval. "But let's be positive."

The more I thought about it, a positive approach was exactly what my son's diving coach was spending time on: mental rehearsal and visualization. "See and feel yourself doing every detailed part of the dive from when you walk toward the board until you hear the crowd's applause as you climb out of the pool." When I told Judy this, she asked, "Does your son ever complain about the water being too cold?"

Rehearse the session in your mind and visualize a positive meeting.

I was ready for the next meeting. I could already feel it being successful. Judy brought me back to reality when she asked, "Roughly how many issues do you plan to bring up with Pat?"

Keep it simple: focus on no more than two issues.

The answer seemed obvious, "Well, all of them of course." For some reason that didn't sound right. Could Pat deal with a lot of things at once? Could I? Could Judy? It seemed so clear in retrospect. I had always advocated doing a couple of things well. Why hadn't I seen that this applied to problem-solving?

I was beginning to feel comfortable about my approach to the meeting, but I still didn't have a clear picture of exactly how to talk with Pat. Judy brushed my thought aside. "Let's talk about your objective for having the coaching session with her."

What were your objectives for the meeting?

"What do you mean objective? I am the manager and there is a problem that has to be solved. It's my job to solve it."

Managers and employees agree that the most important purpose of a coaching session is to develop the employee.

My impatience was beginning to show, but Judy persisted. "But are you there to take disciplinary action, correct an immediate problem, or what?" I hadn't thought very specifically about it, so she had me again. Seeing my discomfort, Judy said, "I've talked to a number of employees and managers about the purpose of a coaching session, and the general consensus is that its purpose is to help the employee.

This had a more positive ring to me than some of the things I had said. If I could keep this in mind before and during any session with an employee, I knew that even sessions focused on specific performance problems would be more productive. "Great," I thought, "now we can get into what I need to do during the actual coaching session?"

"You know what to do to make a session successful."

But Judy sat up and started to leave. Noting the questioning look on my face she said, "I know you want more help, but I believe managers know what to do to make a coaching session successful. The problem is doing it. But if you need to bounce some ideas off of someone, I'd suggest you talk to Roy. We feel he is the best coach in the company."

Roy is the best coach in the company.

I had heard of Roy, but never actually talked to him. He was a Vice President and in a different functional area. As I dialed his number, I had a momentary feeling of embarrassment about asking for help. But his approach on the phone made me more comfortable. He said he didn't have anything written down because each manager's approach is unique. But he has talked with a lot of managers about coaching and would be glad to test my thinking out and see if he could add anything new. I went home that night looking forward to my meeting with Roy.

Tuesday, April 6

The next day, Pat had returned to work and the office was a flurry of side conversations about her trip to the doctor. Luck was with me; I had some morning meetings that kept me from having to deal with the situation. After lunch, I forced myself to go to Pat and see how bad the damage was.

One look told me how much she was suffering. Her eyes revealed that she hadn't slept much, and her cold stare told me that she would have been more pleased to see a mortician at her desk. I cleared my throat and asked her how the doctor's appointment had gone. She immediately said, "That's personal," with a look intended to put me in my place. Small talk wasn't going to cut it so I said, "I would like to have another meeting with you to continue our discussion from the other day." Her face turned red and the muscles in her jaw tightened. I thought for sure that something on her desk would come flying at me; instead she said coldly, "You're the boss."

Setting up the third discussion with Pat

"What a tough cookie," I thought. But I proceeded, " I want to talk about this openly, and I hope we can find a way to make things better. I really am concerned about you and your situation and feel that together we can work something out."

She looked at me and, for a second, I thought she believed me. I had meant it. Then her gaze became more distant, like a curtain closing between us. I quickly interjected, "Let's both think about it for a couple of days, get our facts straight, and meet at 2:00 in my office on Thursday. Okay?" She nodded her agreement, and I felt like a small start had been made.

As I walked away from her desk, I became aware of how quiet the office was. The others on the floor were watching. Pat's problem and my response had become the center of attention, and it looked as if production would continue to suffer until the issue was resolved. My meeting tomorrow with Roy couldn't come too quickly.

Wednesday, April 7

The next day, as I got off the elevator, I noticed Roy

Meeting with Roy

informally talking to a number of his employees. My brief observation suggested a relationship of mutual respect between these people. How much I envied that! As soon as Roy noticed me, he broke off the conversation and escorted me into his office.

"So you want to talk about coaching?"

"Yes, and I hope you can tell me what to do because. . ."

Quietly he interrupted, "I don't plan on telling you anything. I'm hoping we can put what you already know into action. So tell me what you tried to accomplish with Pat during your last meeting."

"I don't plan on telling you anything."

"I haven't given that a lot of thought, but as nearly as I can recall, I tried to get her to see the problem and define a solution."

Smiling he said, "And she wouldn't talk about it and argued with you."

"Right! How did you know?"

"Just a lucky guess," he said. "Then what did you do?"

"I kept trying to get her to see the problem. I guess I must have sounded like a broken record, stating and restating the problem."

"Any luck?"

"Not really!"

"How would you react if I said you shouldn't worry about solving the problem?"

"Don't worry about solving the problem."

"I would say that wouldn't be doing my job."

"True. But what I mean is that during the session, you need to concentrate first on things other than problem-solving."

"Like what?"

Without answering me, he just asked, "Why do you feel comfortable talking to me about your problem with Pat?"

"Well, I think you understand how frustrating this is for me, and you seem to be willing to work with me in figuring this out. Because I like you, I feel it's okay to discuss my problem with you."

Liking me is not the issue.

"Whether you like me is not as critical as an open and trusting relationship."

As I sat thinking about Pat, I noticed a plaque on his wall signed by a number of employees that read,

"Thanks for being supportive."

"Are you saying that I need to make a decision and provide an atmosphere of support before I can attempt to solve problems with an employee?" He just looked at me. After some silence, I acknowledged, 'You know that does make some sense; when I think back, there was a very supportive manager who inspired me to improve my performance." Roy then said that he tried to follow the rule of the third. Before this thought left me, I reached for my note pad.

Roy continued, "There are a number of different things you can do to be viewed as supportive during a counseling session. You have to determine the best and most comfortable way for you. Your supportive actions need to be independent of the employee's support at this point in the game."

Feeling as if I had just walked into a maze, I asked, "But when do I bring up the problem?"

I was startled by Roy's response, "Most employees are aware that a problem exists before you decide to have a conversation with them."

"Are you saying that one way of being supportive is to recognize this and give the employee credit during the conversation?"

"This is really helpful. Can you give me some other ideas of things I need to do to be supportive?" I asked.

"Why don't we just put our heads together and brainstorm a list of supportive behaviors?" he responded. I jotted down a heading on the pad: SUPPORTIVE BEHAVIORS

"Where do we start?" I asked.

Roy sat forward in his chair and said, "Let's think about things which would set the tone or make the overall climate for the meeting supportive. Any ideas?"

"I can think of a few things some of my better managers did. They seemed to hold me in high positive regard and kept our discussion positive, non-threatening, and friendly in tone."

"What do you mean by positive regard?" he asked.

"They seemed to enjoy being associated with me. They liked and trusted me. In fact, one manager in particular often said things like, 'You are a good addition to the department. I enjoy working with you.'"

"Wow, I would feel supported if I worked for a manager like that," he said. "Why don't you add that to your list?"

Rule of the third

During the coaching session, spend two-thirds of your time in supportive behavior and one-third of your time problem-solving.

When do I bring up the problem?

Give the employee credit: 90% of employees are aware a problem exists before your coaching meeting starts.

Supportive behaviors

Talk about positive regard: express acceptance of the employee and the value you place on the association.

"Now, how about the non-threatening tone you mentioned?"

"Yes," I said, "this particular manager was able to keep our discussions positive in tone, even when they were very difficult or involved a difference of opinion. He'd say things like, 'My concern is not to place blame but to solve the problem. I want to make this a constructive conversation and focus on attacking the problem, not each other.'"

Keep the exchange positive: state issues in a gentle, non-aggressive, non-threatening way. Be patient.

"It wasn't just what he said with words. You knew he meant it because he worked so hard during the discussion to make it happen."

"That's super," he said. "That's my intent, but sometimes it seems hard to clearly and believably communicate it to an employee. But, that's what makes this business fun. Let me add one to your list. To me, support is being flexible and making the problem-solving process a joint one between two people and not just a one-way street."

Be collaborative/ flexible: maintain teamwork, mutual problem-solving, and a "let's solve this together" attitude.

"Let me piggyback on that and add the word collaborative. The employee and I need to strive for a 'let's solve this together' attitude."

"I like that," he affirmed.

"Let's get something to drink and keep going," I said. "This is exciting. You really have some good ideas."

As we sat there, a thought occurred to me and I said, "Roy, I would like to get more specific about what actually happens during the session."

"I agree. What are some of your ideas?"

"I often think about how much time I talk and how much time I allow the employee to talk during our meetings."

Share the conversation load: managers should talk no more than 60% of the time.

"That's interesting," Roy said, "I expect the employee to carry 40% of the conversation load. So the 40-60 rule is what I try to live by."

"I noticed that you asked me a lot of questions when we started to talk. It got me thinking and gave me the feeling that you were interested."

"Right," he said.

"Okay, we're on a roll. What's next?"

"How about simply helping the employee?" Roy asked.

"I don't understand."

Become a resource to the employee: provide help, be available, and be willing to try a new way.

"If you can become a resource to the employee, either by providing assistance, being accessible, or being willing to try something new, would this mean anything?"

"You bet," I said, "this would feel better to me than being left alone to resolve the issue."

Then another thought occurred to me, "Don't you also have to be optimistic and believe in the employee's potential?" I asked.

"Absolutely! If you don't communicate confidence and encouragement to the employee, who will?"

"Roy, what bothers me is that I may sound phony or plastic, but I think what helps make this all legitimate is a genuine concern for the employees' interests and objectives. If I am careful to try and protect the employees' rights, help them achieve their objectives, and receive fair consideration, then I shouldn't have to worry about being viewed as phony."

Roy just smiled, "I couldn't have put it any better."

"Roy, you know, every once in a while I think about Pat. She really has had a tough break in her life, and she must feel very upset and used. That's got to be a heavy burden."

Roy smiled, "I don't think you can be supportive without doing what you have just done, walking in the other person's shoes."

"You simply need to treat the employees' feelings and concerns with dignity and give them fair consideration," Roy said. "Another thing I thought of while you were talking is helping employees maintain positive self-esteem. That's a little different from the things you have already listed, but just as important. How do you see that playing out?" asked Roy.

"I think you would have to express appreciation for employees – their knowledge, skills, and abilities. A piece of this would be acknowledging the employees' contribution and role in the work unit."

"And how could I have forgotten this one? Listening to the employee is the highest compliment."

Roy responded, "Listening is really a big part of the 60-40 rule we talked about earlier."

I was starting to run out of ideas when Roy leaned forward and with excitement and said, "How about owning up?"

Puzzled, I said, "Like in a bet?"

"No, like in sharing responsibility for the current state of affairs," Roy responded.

Communicate encouragement and confidence in the employee's potential.

Let employees know you are aware and sensitive to their interests, needs, objectives, and aspirations.

Empathize with the employee's feelings and emotions about the issue or concern.

Maintain the employees' positive self-esteem: tell them they are important and that you value them.

Listen: understand what employees are saying, and give them full consideration and attention.

Own up: share the responsibility for the current state of affairs when appropriate.

"You don't have to do all these things!"

I slid back in my chair to a more comfortable position and yawned, "I am drained of ideas."

"So am I," he said, "but I think you have developed an excellent list for yourself, and I know you can do it. Just remember that you don't have to do all of these things we have talked about in one session and that you do have to be yourself and not use a script."

"Roy, you've been a great help. Would you like a copy of the list?" He smiled and said, "Sure I can add it to the others."

"Others? Are there others?"

"Yes, and I must admit that there is not a significant difference among all the lists I have received copies of over the years. But don't look so defeated. You have created an original for you."

"Why are the lists so similar?" I asked.

"Because coaching is really no mystery. You have to trust yourself to do what you already know."

Managers know what to do during a successful coaching session – the problem is allowing yourself to do it.

"You have to rely on your own list as you put these things into practice during the live session. My hunch is that you can and will do it. I wish you luck."

I felt mentally exhausted but elated. The greatest coach in our company had just helped me understand how I could reach out and connect with Pat. I knew it wouldn't be easy, but I was excited about the opportunities and challenges that my next meeting with Pat would present.

Thursday, April 8

Third discussion with Pat

Thursday morning was dismal. The rain lashed at my office windows, and the sky was a forbidding gray. As Pat entered my office, her cold stare added to the chill. The tension mounted, and I could feel all the confidence and good ideas I had been developing over the past few days fade as quickly as sun behind the clouds. Concerned that the meeting could easily get out of control, I gave myself a quick, silent pep talk. "Get a hold of yourself. Relax. You know what needs to be done, so let's get on with it." I cleared my throat and said, "Pat, I don't imagine you are finding this any more comfortable than I am." Silence. My God, is she going to stare at the floor the whole meeting? Well, there is nothing to do but plod onward. "Let me start. I know things have been tough for you, and I want to help."

"You can help by leaving me alone and telling the rest of your gossipmongers to do likewise," she blurted out.

"Leave me alone."

"I understand you want to be left alone when things are difficult, but you need to know that I can't accept that. The kind of help I can offer you is understanding. You got a raw deal, but now we need to figure out where we can go from here."

I can't accept that.

"What do you know about raw deals? Your life looks pretty comfortable to me."

"Pat, maybe I don't know a lot about raw deals firsthand, but I believe that I can help you move beyond this experience. Something different needs to be done now, and we need to work out what that is." Wow!! The intensity in her look reminded me of a cornered jackal poised for the attack. I knew we were at a critical point – what to say? "Trust yourself," I heard a voice inside me, leading me on. "Pat, if you continue to view me as the enemy rather than as a partner, we're not going to get anywhere."

"Enemy or partner?"

"Well, you're sure not a friend," she shot back.

"Perhaps you don't feel that we can team up again. That's your choice. But I am willing to respect you as a professional employee and to treat you fairly – and that's all I'm asking from you."

The silence was fraught with emotion. A base drum had replaced the clock on my wall. I could hardly hear Pat as she said, "That's all I've ever asked for – to be treated like everyone else. I may have made mistakes, but I'll be damned if I'll give others the satisfaction of gloating over them. To hell with them, all of them! I got myself into this, and I'll get myself out – without any help from you or from them, thank you very much."

"If I didn't really want to help you, Pat, it would be awfully easy for me to say, 'Fine, I am glad you're willing to take care of things, and have a nice day.' I am not going to do that because I feel responsible for some of the things that have happened to you, and I want to play a part in figuring out how we can turn things in this department around."

"I feel responsible."

"Just tell your spies to lay off. If they would quit being so nosy and stop acting like a bunch of old women, things would work themselves out."

"So, Pat, you're saying that it's all their fault?"

"Well, what about Rico? Why just this morning he. . ."

"You have to
change."

"Wait, Pat," I interrupted, "before we talk about Rico. I want you to hear that I am willing to help, but you have to do some things differently here at work, not just depend on Rico and the others to change."

"What if I don't
want to do things
differently?"

"What if I don't want to do things differently, what if I don't want to work here, what if I want my old job back?" she blurted out with an intensity that I had never seen before.

I paused a second and then asked, "Is your old job available?" Her silence answered the question. "As far as your working here, I believe you can play an important part in our group. I want to be as clear and honest as I can about that point."

"I've got to work, I want to work, and I can't afford to start all over again. But I still have my pride left, and I'll be damned if I will give anyone the satisfaction of seeing me crawl. You'll have to fire me first."

"I don't expect you to crawl, and I certainly don't want to fire you. I just want you to do your job in a professional way, using the skills you have with people, the way I've seen you work in the past. You helped me out of some rough spots, and now I want to do the same for you. But you do have coworkers, and your job requires close cooperation with them."

"I know I have shut them out," she sighed. "I guess I was just trying to hurt them, the way they had hurt me. Not one of them helped me when I needed it, especially Rico."

"Let's really look
at this."

"Okay, let's really look at this. Just exactly who have you been hurting?"

"I hope all of them," she said with a glare.

"Why? What have they said to you?"

"They haven't said anything."

"Well, it must really be getting to them then. Let me ask the question again."

Pat's shallow laugh echoed off my walls. "Isn't that ironic? Here I try to get them and wind up hurting myself – what a joke!"

Minutes ticked by, but self-discovery had been key in my growth as an employee, and I wanted the same opportunity for Pat. I wasn't ready for her next outburst.

"How do you expect me to work with these people? Can't you transfer me back to where I was?"

"That's not an alternative, Pat. I think you know that. We need to figure out how to make the best out of your present job." Retreating once more, Pat's gaze returned to the floor. She mumbled a few words that were hard to make out. . . I don't think she wanted me to hear it. I said, "Look, Pat, let's not defeat ourselves before we try. Why don't you tell me why the work in the department is not getting done on time?"

"You tell me why."

She didn't answer right away, but this time I waited, giving her a chance to sort through some of the thoughts and feelings that seemed to be churning inside her. When she spoke again, it was more softly, "That's pretty tough. I mean, isn't it like signing my own death warrant?"

"Pat, if I wanted to fire you I could. I just think that you're smart enough to help me get to the bottom of this."

Her words came more easily now. "I suppose you're right," she said, "but if it's not hurting anyone but me, I'm sort of defeating my own purpose."

"I suppose you're right."

"It's also hurting our team's productivity, but not as much as it's giving you a negative image in the company."

At that, she snapped back, "How much worse can it be?"

"Believe me, I think people have pretty much seen through Bob and aren't dwelling on the past nearly as much as you think. From now on, I would worry about the effect your actions are having on your future."

Pat just smiled and said, "So it appears my withdrawal from the team has slowed up the whole chain of production."

I calmly replied, "You hit the nail right on the head."

"Okay, I can handle the others, but working with Rico. . . he's a real. . . well I won't say it. . I just won't say what I think about him."

"That's where we need to focus our attention. How you get along with your peers is ultimately going to affect what people think of you and whether they cooperate with you. Is there anything that you could do differently?"

"Why don't you talk to him?" Pat pleaded.

I could feel the burden being shifted back to me, but I persisted. "I wouldn't rule that out, but for now, I want to go back to my original question, "Is there anything you can do?"

"What can you do?"

"Okay," Pat said, "I'll talk to him. Isn't that good enough?

I thought that's what you wanted. Why are you looking at me so funny?"

"Because I would like to know more specifically when and how you plan to do this."

After another long silence Pat responded, "I think I'll ask Rico to have lunch and tell him that I want to try and work more closely with him in the future. The only thing I can do then is to see how he responds and whether we can come up with some different things to do. Is that acceptable?"

"For now," I said, "that is a really good start. Do you think you can schedule this sometime this week?"

"So you don't trust me?"

"No, that's not it. I want you to know that I do trust you, but it's important for me to know when I can expect some progress."

"I'll try to get together with Rico in the next two days," she said.

"I think that would be a good start. This won't only help you, Pat, but it will be an important step in helping the entire team be more effective. I know you'll give it your best shot. Why don't we meet after you have lunch with Rico and talk about what happened and how I can help."

There was a lengthy pause. . ."Okay, I appreciate what you are trying to do."

As Pat walked out of the office, I felt a tremendous sense of relief. Our meeting had gone well, not perfectly, but we had made a start. It had taken just short of one hour, but it hadn't seemed as long as our last meeting. Luckily, I didn't have anything else scheduled this time to add extra pressure.

I decided to get a drink of water and then unwind while I reflected on our meeting and captured the key points in my journal. As I turned the corner, Rico about ran into me. "Hey," he said, "heard you were having a meeting with Pat. Sure hope you smoothed things out; it has been a real bummer working with her."

Rico's smile was more cynical than friendly. I wasn't ready for another long discussion, so I brushed him off with, "She'll probably want to talk to you about how the two of you can best work together. I would suggest you take seriously what she has to say."

"Great," he said snidely, "I've been waiting for my chance to work closer with her."

I ignored the cheap innuendo. "Just give her a fair shot at talking to you, Okay?"

"Sure, count on me."

Rico's attitude helped me sense what Pat was confronting constantly, and it was upsetting to say the least. I put my feelings aside temporarily, so that I could focus on capturing some thoughts in my journal while the discussion with Pat was still fresh on my mind. As I took the journal out of my briefcase, I immediately began to feel better. Where to start? Pat's conversation was sincere. I began a new page and titled it: PROBLEM SOLVING.

Okay, so the tone of the conversation had allowed us to look at the problems in a constructive fashion, but there had to be more to it than that. Roy said I would know what to do, but what did I do? As I thought back on the conversation, I felt one of the key priorities had been keeping the conversation channels open between Pat and me.

Pat and I both talked openly about some pretty touchy subjects. But Pat kept raising matters which I felt were irrelevant to the issue at hand and sometimes didn't seem to understand the exact nature of the problem. I remembered thinking at the time that I had to help us keep focused on the problem, even though Pat wanted to take the conversation in different directions.

It seemed to help when I stated my expectations in this situation. Pat seemed to really take note of these.

But beyond that, how could I have forgotten that look in Pat's eye when I told her I wanted her to help me analyze the problem. She seemed pleased that we both had something to contribute to a better understanding of the situation.

Now that I think back on it, this approach did seem to keep us focused and created a team approach to the problem. I guess if I hadn't done this, she might have felt put down, like she wasn't too smart; that would have been extremely difficult. The only other thing that kept us focused was my wanting us both to understand as much about the problem as we could. I was afraid that too many rumors, assumptions, and opinions were floating around, so I wanted us to agree on just exactly what the facts were. I could remember a math professor once saying, "A problem well defined is a problem half-solved."

With both of us thinking and discussing the specifics

Problem solving

Expressing support allows the employee to perceive you as genuinely interested and facilitates a more honest discussion of the problem at hand.

Keep a high level of support and involvement throughout the conversation.

Keep the focus on the problem.

Clarify expectations and needs.

Acknowledge the employee's awareness of the problem.

Define the topic and issues

Establish the impact

behind the problem, we couldn't help but keep focused.

Even though we had defined the problem, Pat still didn't think it was such a big deal. Now I remember it wasn't until we discussed the impact the problem was having on her image and the department that she started to take it seriously. Looking at the impact seemed to be a critical turning point in the conversation.

It made the whole issue more personal and important. What was it my psychology professor used to say? Internalize. Yes, she had started to own the problem. She did a personal value analysis. I felt really excited about this discovery. I sat back for a few minutes and considered this point. If we hadn't discussed the impact, I bet she would have continued to consider the problem mine instead of hers or ours.

Initiate action plans

The conversation seemed to get a little easier from that point on. The next thing we did was to try and determine some specific things that could be done differently. Pretty straightforward, I thought, but the key was we didn't stop until we both felt like we had a good plan developed.

Get a commitment

At the time, I remember thinking, "Is she really going to give this a good try or is she just leading me on?" So I asked her if she was going to try it. Sounds pretty simple, but I wonder how many times in the past I had assumed that an employee would do something – unfortunately too many.

As I think about it now, there were plenty of times when I wanted to get really negative and let Pat know what would happen if she didn't shape up – why didn't I? That's interesting. I guess I never reacted too favorably to what I used to call "doom messages," so I didn't say anything to Pat. Wait a minute, yes I did. I tried to keep it positive and let her know

Emphasize positive consequences

what good would result if she was successful in trying our plan. That didn't seem to hurt; in fact, she seemed to appreciate having some additional reasons for trying to follow through on the plans. I can imagine how she would have reacted if I'd reverted to a more harsh and primitive approach to managing the situation.

My hand hit the glass of water as I put the pencil down, but I caught it before it tipped. I continued to mentally replay the meeting. There were times during the conversation that Pat tried to pass the buck and blame others or her situation for the problem. Every time this happened, it was like a warning flag being waved in front of my face. I knew that if she was permitted to deny responsibility for the problem, she'd never feel ownership for finding a solution. She also tried to give me some reasons why nothing could be done about the current situation. This to me was the same; it kept us from coming up with a solution. I came to realize that excuses and obstacles would only keep us both from coming to grips with the problem and from figuring out a way to deal with it. My approach had to be to listen to the excuse or obstacle she presented and then redirect the conversation to an area we could control – namely, how she behaved.

Confront excuses and resistance

Thinking hard, I could only remember how I tried to end the conversation, wanting to continue to work with her towards improvement and setting up a specific time for review.

Don't give up follow up

Wow! It was a mental struggle to get all that down on paper. It was more tiring than the actual conversation, but I knew my list would be helpful in future conversations with Pat, as well as with other employees. I ended the day with the sense that I had done all that I could. The next step was up to Pat.

Friday, April 9

When Pat bounded into my office the next afternoon, I couldn't believe the difference. She had a grin from ear to ear and a sparkle in her eye that I had forgotten she possessed.

"Just wanted to update you on my lunch meeting with Rico. It was a little difficult at first. I could tell he didn't trust me, so I told him that was okay. I'd prove to him that I could do the job. We talked about ways we could work together, and by the end of lunch, he asked me whether we should continue our discussion over dinner!"

Lunch with Rico

"That's great, Pat! Now you're sounding like the coach. I'm really glad you met with Rico, but you will be cautious about the type of relationship you build, won't you? I'd hate to see Rico turn into another Bob." I grimaced as I recalled Rico's self-centered remarks about Pat. "Perhaps I'd better talk to him."

Pat interrupted my musing with a genuine sense of concern. "I know how this must look to you, but there are still two sides to this story. I know how difficult it is to mix busi-

"There are two sides to this story."

ness with pleasure. If Rico has something other than business in mind, I'll be very clear about what I want. A work relationship that helps both of us do our jobs is what I'm interested in. I appreciate your concern, but I think I'll be okay."

I found it hard to believe this was the same Pat who had caused me so much anxiety. I'd felt our discussion had gone well, but this was a miracle! Maybe, she would be all right. "Thanks for sharing that with me, Pat. I feel more confident now than I ever have before that you're going to be a wonderful asset to the department! Welcome back!"

"Thanks for listening."

Pat just smiled. "Thanks for listening. I think I'd better get back to work. I have a lot of catching up to do."

It all seemed too good to be true, so I kept my eyes on Pat and Rico, and the rest of the department. The atmosphere didn't seem quite real. I'm sure everyone was waiting for some new crisis. But it did seem as if some new efforts at teamwork were being made. Pat and Rico seemed to be working well together, so my heart dropped when Rico asked if he could speak to me privately. I'd been feeling so good. I really wasn't ready to deal with a new problem.

"What is it, Rico? Is there a problem between you and Pat?"

"No. Not at all. I've just been feeling really bad about what I said to you about her. She's not at all what I thought, and her work is doing a lot for this department. I just wanted you to know. . ."

Rico disappeared as quickly as he had come, perhaps a bit embarrassed that he'd let his macho exterior slip for a bit. I just shook my head. Who would have predicted it?

A twist of fate

But the drama and irony of this whole situation wasn't quite over. At dinner that evening, I proudly described to my family how excited I was about my new found leadership success. I must admit I was beginning to feel like I was getting my department back under control. As the evening wore on, I was mentally reviewing my plans for a meeting the next day with the entire department. Just as I began to envision my opening statement, my spouse, who loves to watch the local evening news, yelled at me "Hey, come and see this." As I entered the TV room and looked at the screen I was shocked. Why sure enough, it was Bob, our old Marketing Director, being interviewed by a reporter. "What is he doing on T.V.?" I thought to myself. "I thought he had left town." I turned up the volume and listened intently to the interview. The camera angle changed, and I noticed that two members from our board of directors were also talking to the reporter. "What the heck is going on?" I sat glued to the T.V. Everyone in the room was asking me, "What are they saying? What are they saying?" It seemed like the interview was about a buyout or merger of our company by some new investors. And then the interview was over in a flash. "Merger mania" in the business world has hit the medium-size companies as well as the Fortune 500, I thought. I guess Bob is as well connected in the business world as he said. He must have moved fast after he was fired in order to retaliate and to be able to gather enough investors and force the board members into a sale. From what I heard of the interview, the stockholders will certainly make money on this deal. But it will be pure chaos having Bob as our CEO. Why, he is a marketing man, not a corporate executive, or so it had seemed. The shock of these swift business maneuverings was too much for me to fathom. I retired for the evening, anxious to get to work tomorrow to catch the fall-out.

Bob on T.V.

A merger!!

Bob as C.E.O.

I didn't sleep a whole lot that night. My mind was reeling about the thoughts of the new leadership in our company. When I rushed into the office the next morning, I was anxious to get my group together for the meeting we had planned. I noticed the main floor was alive with activity. Everyone had crowded up to a bulletin board in the main hall that was full of announcements. I planned to go down later and read through them myself, when the crowd had thinned out a little. I probably wouldn't have sensed anything out of the ordinary but the elevator became strangely quiet as I got on, and I felt suddenly uncomfortable; for a minute I thought maybe I had forgotten to comb my hair. When I got to my office, Pat was there waiting for me. Not knowing what else to do, I asked her to come in and sit down. She looked tired and unsettled. I groaned inwardly, wondering what new crisis was upon us. I waited expectantly and finally Pat began.

No sleep tonight

"You haven't heard then?"

"No, I guess I haven't, though people did seem to be acting a bit strange on the elevator," I said.

"Well you better sit down then, this may come as a bit of a shocker." I did as Pat suggested and then she showed me Bob's re-organization announcement for our group. It had Bob's signature on it. I am sure my face went as white as the paper I was reading. "Oh crap," I heard myself saying. Bob was making Pat the director for my department along with two other departments. I was stunned and flabbergasted. Thoughts raced through my mind about how I had been treating Pat during the last few weeks. At first, I thought the worst. "My career is down the tubes . . . maybe I can update my resume."

Woops!! Pat is the new Director

I guess the panic on my face provoked Pat to speak. "Are you all right?"

"Oh, sure, sure, a. . . a. . . congratulations. . . I mean this must be exciting for you. . ." I couldn't think of anything else to say to her.

Pat said, "Thanks. There is something I would like to explain to you. I know this looks like things have happened pretty fast, but you should know that Bob's plans to take over this company were in the works even before he was hired. He told two or three people about his ideas right before he left and swore us to secrecy until he was in the driver's seat with the investors and had the financing together. Bob believed that the CEO was too cautious and traditional and was really holding down the growth potential of the company. I guess they finally had a big argument and blowout. That's why Bob left."

"Holy smokes," I interrupted, ". . . How did you know about all this?"

"Well, Bob seemed to feel that my abilities and drive fit in well with his plans. I guess the chemistry was right."

I couldn't keep up with what Pat was saying. The implications of this change began to settle in. When Pat finished talking she asked me, "How are you doing? You've been pretty quiet."

I took a deep breath. "How will I explain this to my department?"

"What do you mean?"

"I think they will wonder if I am going to keep my job now that you are the boss."

What about me?

Pat was quiet for a minute before she responded, "I want you to know that I need you right where you are. You have taught me a lot about leadership."

"But won't a lot of people be wondering if you will try to get even for the way you've been treated?"

"Well, it has been tough, but I think we need to pick up the pieces and go on together. As the leader of this department, you have my full support."

All I could think about was how close I had come to throwing in the towel with Pat. Now the roles were reversed. I felt more vulnerable and at the same time felt a deep appreciation for the meaning of support and partnership.

Pat's voice broke into my thoughts. "I believe that you had a department meeting scheduled for this morning." I nodded hesitantly. "Let's talk to everyone together. It's going to be important for us to work as a team, and this will be a good place to start."

"Okay, see you at 10:30."

Pat's departure left me with my thoughts. "What a way to go into a weekend. What the heck, I did my best with Pat. No need to look back. This could be interesting."

This could be interesting

Illustration 3.1

3

The Eight-Step Model

INTRODUCTION

Although the story you have just read is fictional, the coaching process is not. It is based on over 18 years of working with leaders in consulting and training programs and on an extensive organizational research effort. Specifically, we and our colleagues have observed and surveyed 50,000 managers and more than a quarter of a million employees on this subject between 1980 and 1998. In addition, an in-depth study, completed in 1986 by Stowell, compared the behaviors of highly effective coaches and their employees to those of less effective coaches and their employees. The data from this study produced 47 categories of leader behavior that play a role in the success of a coaching session. This information has been condensed for the practicing leader. Many of the main conclusions were presented in the preceding fictional account. In the remainder of the book, the information collected from observations, surveys, and research analysis is presented in a more classical way.

We will begin, then, with an Eight Step Coaching Model that represents much of what we have learned about the coaching process. (See Illustration 3.1.) These eight steps serve as a communication road map. In subsequent chapters, supporting coaching concepts will clarify other key leadership behaviors needed to make the Eight Step Coaching Model successful.

STEP ONE: BE SUPPORTIVE

Simply put, supportiveness is not an option when it

"Support is a decision, not an emotional exchange."

comes to coaching. The success of a coaching discussion with an employee about needed changes or improvements to performance is determined by the employee's perception of the leader's supportiveness. No other factor is as important as this. The highly effective leaders that we studied devoted half of their time and attention to expressing some sort of supportive message. They were basically able to do two things: (1) express this apparently unconditional positive support very clearly to the employee, and (2) initiate a strong and clear problem-solving discussion without being punitive or demeaning to the employee.

In all likelihood, this step is not a surprise to most people. Many coaching models include this step in one way or another. However, the fact that it is such a significant and dominant step is a key discovery. Support and the strong emphasis that we give it constitutes the most distinguishing feature of our coaching process. This step has been placed at the center of our model. It symbolically touches all of the other steps because highly effective leaders express support as they move through the problem-solving process (represented by the outer ring of steps). Any one coaching session can contribute to the employee's overall perception of the leader's willingness to be supportive. Supportiveness needs to precede the discussion and should be continued once the coaching session is over. Our evidence demonstrates that supportiveness must be a long-term effort.

The level of support employees attribute to managers is a matter of degrees. Employees always have a perception about the supportiveness of their managers. Because managers have no option – this perception cannot be avoided – the wise manager seeks to engage in behaviors that result in being viewed as supportive. To improve your effectiveness as a coach, increase the level of support as perceived by the employee.

But how do you show that you are supportive? You have a number of choices. The effective managers we studied paid attention to the quality of the relationship and did things to maintain a healthy exchange. These managers engaged in ten distinct caring behaviors:

TEN SUPPORTIVE BEHAVIORS

Collaboration/ Flexibility

COLLABORATION/FLEXIBILITY:

Responsibility is mutually shared for assignments, tasks, and changes, with a willingness to compromise and work together.

HELPING/ASSISTING:

The leader is willing to help out, provide resources, and be available for future consultation.

Helping/
Assisting

EMPATHY/UNDERSTANDING:

The leader treats the employee's feelings, concerns, obstacles, and difficulties with dignity.

Empathy/
Understanding

RECOGNITION OF EMPLOYEE'S VALUE:

The leader expresses appreciation, believes the employee is an important part of the team, and contributes to the employee's positive sense of self-esteem.

Recognition of
Employee's Value

LISTENING/INTERACTION:

The leader is willing to give the employee his/her full attention by asking a lot of questions and giving the employee time to express ideas, reactions, and suggestions.

Listening/Interaction

RECOGNITION OF EMPLOYEE'S INTERESTS/GOALS:

The leader is aware of the employee's interests, individual needs, objectives, and aspirations.

Recognition of
Employee's
Interests/Goals

POSITIVE FEEDBACK/CREDIT:

The leader is willing to point out successes and give the employee credit for specific past achievements.

Positive
Feedback/Credit

ENCOURAGEMENT/OPTIMISM:

The leader is hopeful, reassuring, and of the belief that the situation can be solved as a result of the employee's efforts.

Encouragement/
Optimism

POSITIVE EXCHANGE:

The leader's friendly approach focuses on issues in a gentle, non-aggressive, non-threatening, non-judgmental way.

Positive Exchange

OWNING SOME RESPONSIBILITY/OPENNESS:

The leader accepts responsibility for contributing to the situation and doesn't blame it all on the employee. They share important information and insight, and the leader shows trust.

Listed in Illustration 3.2 are the ten most common sup-

Owning Some
Responsibility/
Openness

portive behaviors. Although not a strict ordering, the most important behavior is collaboration/flexibility.

Illustration 3.2

The Hierarchy of
Supportive Leader Behaviors

1. COLLABORATION/
FLEXIBILITY

2. HELPING/
ASSISTING

3. EMPATHY/
UNDERSTANDING

4. RECOGNITION OF
EMPLOYEE VALUE

5. LISTENING/INTERACTION

6. RECOGNITION OF EMPLOYEE'S
INTERESTS/GOALS

7. POSITIVE FEEDBACK/CREDIT

8. ENCOURAGEMENT/OPTIMISM

9. POSITIVE EXCHANGE

10. OWNING SOME RESPONSIBILITY/OPENNESS

In our studies, we have found that when a leader neglects these behaviors or does the opposite by harsh, aggressive, and non-supportive comments and actions, the employee develops a perception that the leader is not a partner and, in fact, is non-supportive or even adversarial. One other detail we have noticed is that effective coaching experiences correlated highly with the leader and employee having a history of working well together and viewing each other in a positive light.

Hey, I'm not caring!

Some people may look at this and say, "Hey, I am just not a caring and supportive type of person." This creates a special challenge to be more conscious and deliberate in expressing some support during and after a coaching session. Other people may look at this step, dismiss it, and say in a sarcastic tone, "I get loved at home." No matter how much people choose to deny it, a little support at work, especially from the boss, feels incredibly good and certainly contributes to one's self-confidence and self-esteem. These are important elements when things are not going well or when the leader wants to bring about change. It may be that higher level managers feel more cared for and valued by the organization than middle and lower level members of the organization (because of their status, perks, and creature comforts), but don't be deceived by these physical trappings of support. Recognize that expressions of support will be interpreted as helpful at all levels in the organization.

Just to be clear, we are not saying that people in your organization have to "like" you. We are not talking about the leader receiving support and caring behaviors; we are talking about the leader's willingness and courage to give support even in the face of adversity, disappointment, and problems. This is what makes leadership a challenge: to move off and beyond the concern or problem and to enlist the support and cooperation of others as effectively and rapidly as possible. Even though you may have feelings of frustration or even anger, you will need to let them go in order to enlist the genuine willingness and commitment of your employees to make your unit better. If you feel the employee pulling back or withdrawing, you will need to be persistent in clarifying your supportive intentions. You may even want to make your intentions and the employee's resistance a focal point of the conversation for a time in order to build a supportive base.

STEP TWO: DEFINE THE TOPIC AND NEEDS

Step 2 is the first substantive problem-solving step. The purpose of Step 2 is to create a mutually understood picture of what's happening. When giving feedback and discussing the concern or developmental opportunity with the employee, you may find a few tips helpful:

1. Don't start with an accusation. . .that will create a head-on collision, instant defensiveness, and an argument. ("You were really lousy at handling questions in that meeting.") Begin with a more natural introduction. ("I want to talk about the way you handle questions in meetings.")

2. Give the employee some "air time," time to react, vent,

Feedback almost always feels personal: "You know you're ugly and your Mom dresses you funny."

TIPS:
Don't accuse

Allow employees "air time"

or defend. All the employee wants you to do is acknowledge that "it isn't easy being an employee" and that "it's a real jungle out there." If the employee does seem a bit defensive say, "I can tell that you have had some difficulties, challenges, obstacles, etc." This will be seen as supportive.

Be specific, descriptive, non-hostile

3. State your concern or issue in a specific, descriptive, non-hostile way. Focus on relevant here-and-now topics. Offer your observations and data. Take ownership for the situation. A vital issue, and one that a lot of well-meaning leaders miss, is that you need to be prepared to accept some responsibility for the current situation as well. Acknowledge that it is very possible that your own actions or omissions may have helped create part of the problem. A lot of leaders play a game: "It isn't my fault. Don't blame me." Work and jobs are complex these days, and it would be very foolish to blame it all on the employee.

"Everyone is responsible and no one is to blame."

Gather employee input

4. Use the time in Step 2 to gather additional data from the employee. Build your understanding of the situation with any specific information or insight that the employee can provide. Be on the lookout for preliminary excuses and justifications. Excuses are normal and natural when a leader questions or doubts the effectiveness of an employee's behavior. They indicate that the employee is beginning to deal with some uncomfortable or harsh realities. All employees want to avoid this anguish and so they try to ignore the issue or offer excuses for their behavior. It's perfectly normal. The leader needs to support this with some understanding and then move on to the rest of the steps.

Restate your information

5. Simply restate your information and interpretation of the issue you want to discuss. If you have planned well, you will have gathered some reliable firsthand data that will be believable to the employee and will make all other data sound like "hearsay" evidence. Remember, too, that this discussion is another step in the information-gathering process. If you don't treat the employee's information with dignity and respect, the employee will believe that your judgment is set in concrete. If the employee has information that you can trust, then respond authentically. Remember that a problem well defined is half solved.

Clarify expectations

6. Next it is very important that you state or restate your expectations – What it is that you "want." The hard/measurable side sounds like a business mission or goal statement,

and the softer side includes a statement of your values and the positive things that you are trying to create in your department. This represents the unique contribution you and your group can make to the company. This is a future-oriented statement that could include functional values (quality, customer relations, accuracy, or creativity), or it could include personal values and wishes (growth, satisfaction, recognition, skill building, or risk taking). The point is to let others around you know what you are working toward and what is important to you in both the short and long run. An example might be, "I expect everyone in our unit to act like a team player and share information as quickly as possible."

The objective of this step is to achieve mutual understanding and to allow both leader and employee perceptions to be expressed. Leaders should try to make this a non-evaluative and descriptive review of the opportunities or concerns. This step should focus on relevant here-and-now issues and not deal with historical performance issues. The leader is making an error by discussing events in the distant past. It is critical that leaders be specific, assertive, and fair to themselves as well as to the employee. The manager can really prepare the employee for change by beginning with good information and gathering additional data from the employee.

Some leaders love this step and find it very easy. Unfortunately, some even take delight in criticizing the performance of others. Other managers find this step extremely difficult and awkward because its confrontive nature can create some anxiety and controversy. The suggestions offered here provide leaders who are either overly aggressive or timid an alternative for presenting the issue and giving feedback.

It is unmistakably clear that leaders should deal with essentially one issue at a time in the coaching session and not commit the "overload" error that is discussed in Chapter 5. The leader can achieve greater success by breaking monumental issues apart and generating some momentum on a manageable piece. We also believe that, at this early stage in the coaching sequence, it is not important for the employee to be in total agreement with your perceptions. Don't push too hard and expect the employee to give in. After all, it is the employee's effort and actions that are being examined

Concentrate on one issue

here, and time is needed to assimilate your points.

Finally, the key things you can do to communicate adequate supportiveness during this step are to listen; clarify your intentions (that you are not here to rake the employee over the coals or chew him/her out); ask questions; acknowledge employee difficulties, excuses, reasons, and justifications when they come up (without bending over and letting the employee off the hook); own up to your share or contribution to the problems; and point out things that are going right. Once this has been done, you can gently start discussing Step 3.

STEP THREE: ESTABLISH IMPACT

Think of Step 3 as the lubricant for the slow-moving gears of change. This step explains why the employee should consider revising his/her action or approach. Step 3 is a vital transitional step in moving from the issue or concern to the forward-looking action and commitment steps. Step 3 is like a hinge or linking pin. Through Step 3 you start to develop the genuine and deep cooperation of the employee.

Benefits (+)	Costs (-)

The intent of Step 3 is to help the employee fully assess and make value judgments about any adverse impact that his/her actions are having on personal goals, the organization's operations, or other individuals and co-workers. By asking the employee to step back from the situation and evaluate the adverse impact, or by clearly stating the negative effects of the employee's actions to this point, you are creating an imbalance, doubts, and disruptions in the employee's mindset about the value of the current course of action. The more this tension or questioning is self-created by the employee, the more interested and ready the employee will be to entertain a discussion of other alternatives.

Step 3 is designed to create the self-motivation to sustain the change process. The energy essential to take action will result when the employee examines the situation and sees how his/her actions are working counter to valued or desired goals, objectives, intentions, and results. This is a tension-raising and complacency-disturbing process that sparks the search for new plans and actions. A good analogy of how Step 3 works is when you look in the mirror after you have over-indulged during a long holiday, and you discover an extra layer of flesh protruding from your body that must go.

Complacency-disturbing

As a leader, you act as the mirror and facilitate the employee's discovery and awareness.

This step is crucial because often the employee has a blind spot or is unable to see the full range of effects of actions. With this step, the leader is simply trying to heighten the employee's awareness of the rest of the world (i.e., customers, top management, co-workers, the leader, careers, other departments, the bottom line, etc.). The best way for the leader to create impact and employee self-awareness is to establish a very vivid example. Ask penetrating questions about the costs and benefits of the employee's current actions or actually create an experience outside of the coaching discussion. These things can be done by engaging the employee in some role reversal with you, customers, or other departments. The leader can ask the employee to do a mental re-evaluation of his/her means to reach certain ends. The leader can make an assignment which will bring the employee into direct contact with the problem or issue (up close and personal). Once this comes into focus, the employee will want to forge on with a new course of action.

Look at blind spots

"The success or failure of the action plan is most often determined by this step."

Our survey data and firsthand observations strongly suggest that this step, more than any of the others, is neglected and avoided. We suspect that leaders underrate the value of some discussion in this area and are in a rush to get on with Step 4 and a plan, or they are not sure how to use this step to achieve its full value.

When the leader has elected to engage the employee in a positive motivational or developmental coaching discussion, this step becomes a powerful solidifying or reinforcing step for behavior that is desired. The leader simply focuses on the positive impact the employee's actions are having on the employee, the organization, or other people.

Managers are sometimes puzzled because this step seeks to create a "pinch" and some internal stress in an effort to unfreeze the employee's thinking and position on the issue raised by the leader. That may seem on the surface to be very non-supportive. We want to be clear about this. We are not advocating psychological torture, nor are we suggesting that you lay a heavy "guilt trip" on the employee. There is a real choice here about how heavy you want to be. We highly recommend that you start with some questions and allow the employee to discover and see the impact. Your questions may seem obvious and redundant to you. . .ask them anyway, and get a feel for how the employee is assessing the situation. Your best hope in communicating support for the employee is to ask, listen, and add to what the employee says. After doing that, you can recap with some direct statements and clarify again that your primary aim is to help the employee learn and grow, despite the fact that some self-realization may be a bit painful at first. Remember, change is sometimes preceded by an abrupt awakening and discovery.

Change=
awakening and
discovery

STEP FOUR: INITIATE A PLAN

Step 4 feels comfortable for most leaders because it sounds solid and positive. In fact, Step 4 is critical because it does represent "pay dirt," "the end zone," or the "bull's eye." Steps 1, 2, and 3 are the building blocks, but this is the place where the actual changes get worked out.

What	When	Where	*How much*

In this step, the manager has a choice of creating and giving a plan to the employee or developing and negotiating a plan with the employee. Unfortunately, a lot of managers feel a strong need at this point to take control of the situation, dictate a plan to the employee, and then ask for a commitment to the manager's plan. We urge leaders to relax their need for control and to think of themselves as catalysts, organizers, and facilitators in jointly developing solutions with the employee, not figuring out the solution for the employee. Obviously, the choice depends on the employee's ability and willingness to respond and to really understand the impact of what's being done. If at all possible, the employee should be involved in making the plan. Using the employee's knowledge of the situation, as well as his/her creativity and talent, to develop a workable plan, will help ensure success. Remember that collaboration is the highest form of support. So if you want to build a partnership with your employee, be as collaborative as the situation will allow.

Involve the
employee

Regardless of who constructs the plan, it needs to be specific, simple, clear, and feasible; in addition, it needs to have timetables. In short, once the discussion on Step 4 has ended, the leader and employee need to be able to say who will do what, where, when, and how much.

Specific, simple,
clear, and feasible

Goals need to be set and clearly understood. Numerous studies have found that clear, difficult, specific goals work

Set goals

better than vague, easy-to-achieve goals. The manager needs to take the lead in making sure clear goals are established, because it is hard for an employee to hit a target that hasn't been set. Then, as much as possible, the manager should encourage the employee to provide ideas on how to reach the goals. The more input from the employee on the plan, the more likely the employee will feel part of the plan and will take ownership for results. As an outgrowth of working together, the employee's personal credibility and judgment, as well as the manager's, are on the line. This will help ensure that the plans are fulfilled.

"You can't hit a target that you don't set."

A lot of managers assume that if they have given the employee clear feedback in Step 2, and if they have helped the employee assess the impact from all the different angles in Step 3, then the employee can construct a specific action plan alone. This is a dangerous assumption. Regardless of who comes up with the plan, the manager has the responsibility to ensure that clear plans are in place. Specific actions must have been laid out and clear timetables established.

STEP FIVE: GET A COMMITMENT

Once a plan has been defined, it is easy to make the mistake of not following through and soliciting clear intentions from the employee, of not articulating and literally asking for a commitment. By using clear and pointed words and questions, the manager is looking for a response from the employee that indicates a willingness and obligation to respond positively, that reveals ownership and responsibility, and that shows the employee does truly believe that the plan can be accomplished as constructed. Therefore, this step is designed to "lock up" a commitment to try the plan.

An employee may feel that the manager is encroaching on his/her freedom. Leaders may need to clarify to the employee that the intent is not to encroach, but to clearly understand and solidify the employee's intentions. It is important to be persistent, to get a clear answer, and to hear the employee actually verbalize a commitment. The manager simply cannot assume or hope that things will change and that plans will be implemented.

Employee's intentions

This step, then, is designed to tie it all together. It's a way to close the deal. Step 5 doesn't take a lot of time. It does take some courage on the manager's part to ask for commitment and to be clear in letting the employee know you are serious.

Some people ask why Steps 4 and 5 are not combined. The reason is that in our research, we found that many managers assume that a commitment is there because a plan was built. Failure to gain a commitment often makes the difference between success and failure. We have kept this step separate in order to give it appropriate emphasis.

"The test of your work is whether the employee does something."

The key in Step 5 is to get a commitment and to initiate the first and most elementary step of the plan immediately. Don't let the employee sit around. When the employee leaves the meeting with you, he/she should be doing some positive act, regardless of its size, that will get the ball rolling.

Ask for it

There are a thousand ways to ask for a commitment: "Will you try it?" "What do you think?" "Can you get behind this plan?" "When can you start?" "What could be done right now to begin?" "Do you think this will work?" It doesn't work to tell the employees to be committed. This has to be voluntary; you need to ask for it. The employee's response will give you vital clues regarding your need to monitor. The commitment step will signal any hesitation and whether the employee is saying "I can't" (due to a lack of knowledge, skill, or ability) or "I won't" (because of a belief that the plan won't work or because of a lack of motivation to change).

STEP SIX: CONFRONT EXCUSES AND RESISTANCE

If applied incorrectly, this step could be interpreted by the employee as non-supportive. The main thrust is for the manager to convey a real determination to act on the plan without being insensitive, harsh, or unreasonable. The firm part of this step is saying to the employee that inactivity simply will not be accepted. The supportive part of this step is saying it is okay to have excuses and reservations and to express them to a leader who will listen and work with the employee to solve them. In designing the model, this step was difficult to place in the eight-step wheel because excuses can develop at any point in the interaction process.

"It's not my fault."
"It doesn't apply to me."
"No one told me."
"I didn't mean it. I was just practicing."

However, as we did more investigating, we found that managers need to take two kinds of excuses into account. The first usually occurs as a result of discussion on Step 2, "Define the Topic and Needs." Those excuses are designed to justify why things are happening the way they are. Although these can be distracting or annoying, they really don't do a lot of harm since they are part of the past. We refer to these as Type I excuses.

Type I Excuses

The other kind of excuse is that which surfaces when future plans and actions are being discussed. These excuses are the ones that create real problems for managers. For that reason, we place this step right after the planning and commitment step. These Type II excuses can submarine or threaten the plan and interfere with future progress.

Type II Excuses

Some people have a little trouble understanding why such a step should be necessary once a commitment has been made. We have found that when there is hesitation, resistance, or a weak commitment to the plan, managers usually begin to see excuses develop at this point in the discussion. Some resistance or excuses are normal, natural, and to be expected when seeking a change from the employee. If the employee is placed in a new situation or asked to try new plans and approaches, the change has the potential of creating a sense of exposure or feelings of being out of control.

Because these kinds of excuses develop as a result of planning and commitment seeking, they pose serious potential threats to the action plan. The challenge here is to get the discussion back on track and moving in a positive, forward direction. The job of the manager is not to focus on the excuse, but rather to get the employee to concentrate on positive actions, contingencies, or back-up plans if problems materialize.

Excuses can be helpful

It may be useful to point out that in some instances excuses can be helpful. They can provide an opportunity for the manager and the employee to foresee problems and do better contingency planning. The hope is that the manager can redirect the employee's thoughts and energy into realistic plans that aren't prone to obstacles and excuses. We strongly suggest that, even if it looks like the employee isn't going to offer any excuses or resistance, the leader take initiative with this step. The leader can do this by going on the offensive and literally asking the employee about any reservations regarding the plan. If the answer is no, this can be pursued further by asking the employee to anticipate or foresee any possible obstacle or reason that the plan might not work and to suggest steps that could be taken now to prevent these conditions from occurring.

Managers shouldn't get bogged down in debates and arguments with their employees. The key is to get some constructive change started. If there are excessive excuses, one approach might be to simplify the plan. The manager should convey the expectation for change to occur and for cooperation from the employee, even if it means reducing the size of the plan.

Since excuses and resistance are mechanisms to insulate employees from dealing with a harsh reality that requires change, give the employees some support and indicate that you know it's difficult. Tell your employee that they are talented, you have faith in them, you are willing to support them, and you do expect some change to happen.

Focus on what can be done

The task of the manager in this step is to get the employee to focus less on excuses and reasons why things won't work and more on what can be done. Talk about what is within the influence and control of the employee, what bits and pieces are controllable. The manager can ask the employee what he/she can contribute in a constructive vein and what he/she is willing to do. The employee needs to see that the manager intends to confront resistance and excuses

Inactivity is not accepted

and is not willing to accept inactivity.

If Steps 1 through 5 are done well, it's not likely that a lot of excuses will emerge. Regardless of whether there are few or many, it may be appropriate to move to Step 7.

STEP SEVEN: CLARIFY CONSEQUENCES DON'T PUNISH

Look to the future

Step 7 creates some unique dilemmas or concerns for the leader. First of all, during a conversation about performance, the manager wants to be clear without being overbearing about the outcomes for the employee if a plan is or is not implemented. Second, our research supports the idea that positive consequences have more impact than negative ones. Third, the manager needs to know when the consequences being discussed are viewed as punishment.

Positive consequences have more impact

Of all the 8 steps, "Clarifying Consequences" represents a dual-edged sword. One edge, the appropriate edge, will result in the employee clearly understanding the outcomes and in solidifying the employee's commitment to give the agreed-to plan a valiant try. The other edge, the punitive side, will result in feelings of resentment and resistance from the employee, together with the recognition that the manager's power and authority – and not the employee's commitment – are the critical drivers for the plan.

To help the manager stay on the appropriate edge, we offer the following ideas. First, use Step 7 with some discretion. The key is to assess the strength of the employee's commitment. If it is weak, the employee needs to understand the negative outcomes that will automatically occur if the plan fails. If it is strong, either forget the negative consequences or mention a few positive outcomes that the employee will experience by succeeding with the plan. Often this whole step can be omitted because the manager and employee have developed a plan that has elicited the commitment and effort required to make it succeed.

IDEAS:
Use discretion

Second, emphasize the positive. This may seem to go against common sense – don't you get better results by scolding your children? But negative consequences were found to "repel," while positive consequences were found to attract the employee into wanting to give the plan an honest chance for success.

Emphasize the positive

Third, try to describe the consequences as natural outcomes that anyone could expect to occur as a result of doing or not doing the plan. These are really natural conditions like laws of nature or society. Don't let the employee think that he/she has been singled out for special negative or positive consequences. For example, any sales person who fails to meet with key decision makers can expect to close fewer sales and have lower sales commissions. These are natural consequences, not unique to any one person. If the person you are coaching doesn't accept or agree with the natural consequences, then you need to describe those that you, as a leader, can impose administratively (types of job assignments, performance ratings, salary adjustments, training opportunities, etc.). These imposed consequences represent the heavy artillery in coaching and should be used judiciously.

Focus on natural outcomes

Fourth, as in Step 3, those consequences that are relative to the employee's personal goals or objectives carry more motivational weight than administrative consequences that can be imposed by the manager.

Relate them to personal goals

Keep this step in perspective. It is critical when you need to increase the employee's commitment and add motivational incentives to the plan. Don't use the negative consequences if they are not needed. Use positive consequences as often as you can, and keep them genuine. If the issue doesn't get resolved after the first or second coaching attempt, then you will want to increase the intensity and clarity of this step. The employee needs to know where he/she stands on the "playing field" and how close that is to being "out of bounds." This step is designed to be informational so that if, later on, it becomes necessary to administer the consequences, the employee won't feel "ambushed" or surprised by the leader's actions. The good news about Step 7 is that it works. The bad news is that it is potent and you can "overkill" with it.

STEP EIGHT: DON'T GIVE UP

During the meeting

Think of this step occurring in two different time frames. The first is during the conversation with the employee, and the second is after the meeting.

During the meeting, this step illustrates your commitment to the employee. You have asked the employee to commit to a plan of action. Your commitment is to discuss and work through the other seven steps with the employee until both of you are comfortable. This means that you must trust the process and have the "supportive toughness" not to let either yourself or the employee off the hook until all seven steps have been fully discussed, or until a plan has been established as to when the remaining steps will be covered. Two excellent leader behaviors illustrate your attention to this step. One is to establish a precise date, time, and location to meet again and follow up on progress. The other is, during the final stages of the meeting, take the initiative to verify, rehearse, review, or ask the employee to review one final time the next steps that the two of you will be taking.

A frequently asked question is how long do you work with the employee or when it is okay to give up. An answer that is hard to quantify but serves as a useful guideline is "longer than the employee expects you to." Employee resistance to execute the plan or hesitation to talk openly about any one of these steps may in fact be a test: "Are the motives of this manager sincere and honest?" "Does my manager really care and want to spend the time it will take to help me change?"

You have to, through your persistence and actions, indicate that you are committed to solving this problem with the employee. So ask those additional questions or make those additional statements when you feel the most frustrated and want to end the meeting. It will take only a few extra minutes and could send the strong message that you are serious and that the employee is not going to get around discussing this as easily as has been done in the past.

This level of commitment takes courage and patience, plus a willingness to devote the time. A lack of willingness to devote the time may indicate that the problem is not that important to you – there are few quick fixes.

After the session, your follow-up actions become an important indicator of your willingness not to give up. It is interesting that in our research, employees more than managers desired extra contact to discuss their performance. Employees predicted that this would have a positive impact on their productivity. On the other hand, they felt their managers were reluctant to engage in these discussions either on an initial or continual basis. The highly effective coaches we studied had more frequent contact with their employees to discuss their performance than did the less effective coaches.

After the meeting

The question that needs pondering is how accessible and available you are to review progress and change the agreed-to plan after the employee gains some experience with trying to implement it. We find many leaders who operate under the notion that discussing a concern equates to solving it. Time pressures and other things frequently demand our attention. This may be an additional obstacle the employee sets up to test your commitment. "Will you follow up, or can I ignore our agreements because you won't bring them up again?"

The message is clear: if you invested the time and energy in getting the employee to understand the problem and plan a course of action, you need to invest some definitive time for follow-up. These follow-up sessions are often the most valuable because now it is you and the employee discussing the plan and how to make it work better, or how to make the partnership work better. The focus is on renewing commitments and revising plans, and away from the employee. All your good work and intentions could be wasted for the want of a series of brief review meetings to evaluate progress or needed changes.

SUMMARY NOTE: APPARENT CONTRADICTIONS

Apparent contradiction?

After initial exposure to the Eight Step Coaching Model, some leaders are a little bewildered and slightly puzzled at the idea of being a strong supporter of the employee, and also knowing that they need to initiate a rigorous problem solving discussion. Sometimes, these contradictions drive leaders away and discourage them from learning how to manage the apparent contradiction. However, the effective leader supports and empathizes with an employee, then presses on and initiates the problem solving process. The effective leader has the ability to be firm and fair, to push at the right time, and yet to be flexible at the appropriate moment. These themes are really embedded in our data and reinforce the support-initiate concept in coaching.

The challenge

"Remember each coaching session is an opportunity to act out the type of partnership you want to create."

We challenge leaders to look closely at this coaching model. On the surface, it may appear that we are asking the leader to do two opposing strategies (be kind. . .then stick it to them) or a sandwich technique (first some good news, next some bad news, then cap it with some more good news). These techniques represent manipulation and deception in its purest form. We believe that the leader's approach can be deeply genuine and needn't come across as a mixed or confusing message. The support-initiate model simply suggests that change in employee behavior is born out of your ability to be caring and interested, as well as the need to have a role in guiding and directing employee efforts. At times, when organizational needs interfere with or limit the flexibility and freedom of individuals, conflict will emerge. However, if you trust the process outlined here, you will be able to work through difficult times.

The Five Levels of Coaching

During our workshop we often ask participants, "When do you coach others?" After listening to numerous specific times and places, someone invariably states, "All the time." Although we believe this to be true, we have tried to be more specific about different levels of coaching. Does the application of the Eight-Step Coaching Model change as these levels change? We believe it does. The purpose here is to explore the five levels and how the Coaching Model can best be adapted to each of them.

The following diagram depicts the five fundamental coaching levels:

Choosing
Level 5

Confronting
Level 4

Mentoring
Level 3

Reviewing
Level 2

Linking
Level 1

GENERAL OBSERVATIONS ABOUT THE STAIR-STEP LEVELS

Spend time on each level.

Symbolically these stair steps reinforce at least four things. First, as a coach, you earn your "rights" to go to the next level only if adequate amounts of time and attention have been spent on the previous levels. Climbing the staircase requires that you spend time on each of the levels. Those you coach will feel blind sided if you move to Level 4: Confronting, without adequate attention to the earlier stairs and your efforts will be frustrating, at best.

Second, the intensity, emotionality, patience, courage to coach, and coaching skills increase at each corresponding level. Just concentrating on the two extremes makes it easy to envision how dramatically different conversations are at Level 1 and Level 5.

Third, the width of each level illustrates how your total coaching time and attention should be allotted. The most time should be spent on linking, next on reviewing, then mentoring, followed by confronting problems. Finally, the least time should be spent on choosing. In reality, all too often, coaching time is spent disproportionately on confronting. Or, other opportunities are missed and concerns arise when something becomes a major problem.

Lastly, these levels are not independent of one another. If the word "problem" is defined expansively, then mentoring is similar to working on a problem. In the process of reviewing, you also are linking. Yet, at times these five levels are unique and independent. The following focuses on distinguishing elements when they are the sole purpose of discussion.

LEVEL 1: LINKING

Bond

Your goal: To build a trusting relationship by knowing the other person, valuing his or her uniqueness, and disclosing your personal side. An overused but useful synonym is bonding. The focus of your interaction is on getting to know the other person and allowing that person to know you at a deeper level than just job title and function. It is a time for mutual appreciation and affirmation of value. One Vice President summed it up best when she said, "We just don't know each other very well, and therefore our discussions are pretty formal and not very deep. We haven't found the synergy or comfort level with one another."

When this is appropriate: Good coaches constantly recognize that the strength of the relationship they have with others is more important than any technique. Trust is built on familiarity, consistency, predictability, and mutuality of goals and interests. Relationships are built through time.

Relationships are built through time.

In 1995 at the age of 34, Rich Neuheisel became the youngest coach of a perennial top 10 college football team, the University of Colorado Buffaloes. Before spring practice he, with the entire team, assistant coaches, and trainers, spent three days camping and experiencing various outdoor exercises including rock climbing and river rafting. The critics called this "camp laid-back"[1]. For Rick Neuheisel it was a way of building links between him, the staff, and the team.

For him, establishing this foundation of familiarity, or linking with one another, was critically important before concentrating on play books, game plans, weight training, and physical conditioning. Too radical when combined with his playing guitar and singing solos of popular rock songs at pre-game pep rallies? Any more radical than Sally Mattei, who supervises 750 EDS employees? "I meet with my direct reports every Monday morning, and we start out listening to a piece of music, generally something calming or reflective. We're silent. We just listen to the music. This week it was a piano solo called 'If You Believe.' It's a pensive, reflective piece of music that makes you sentimental and feel hope for your future. We are whole people, not someone in our private life and someone in our public life. That's what I want in the workplace."[2] (Fortune, October 14, 1996, "This Tough Guy Wants To Give You A Hug"). We would argue that far from radical, these people are keeping things in proper perspective.

Dominant steps in the Coaching Model: Step 1, Be Supportive. When we ask others to tell us about the "best" leaders they ever worked for, we hear, "They were genuinely interested in me as a person, they cared and were concerned about me, they spent time with me, and they were more of a friend or colleague than a manager or boss." The foundation for this is a willingness to share personal expectations, goals, and objectives and to spend time getting to know one another and valuing each person as an individual. Empathy, listening, acceptance, and collaboration are all supportive behaviors that build and maintain a relationship with others.

Additional efforts needed: A personal commitment is needed to spend the time getting to know the people around you and being willing to disclose your own personality and uniqueness to them.

A valuable investment

Some may view this as idle time; we view it as a valuable investment. Our coaching skills trainer refers to this as "building a positive balance in my bank account with others." The additional adjective we hear when people describe their "best" leader/coach is "friend." What's your bank account balance? Could you make a withdrawal without damaging the relationship? When was the last time you made a deposit?

LEVEL 2: REVIEWING

Your goal: To review the status of current activities and explore in a proactive way any concerns of either party. It is a time to exchange views, assumptions, and perceptions of how things are proceeding with regard to current projects and job responsibilities. The coach has the responsibility for proactively initiating and scheduling these discussions.

When this is appropriate: These are normal time-outs to touch base, check progress, and address minor issues before they become major issues. They come in various guises including project reviews, updates, interim reviews, walk throughs, joint sales calls, etc.

A standard operating procedure for Federal Express is that all managers in Ground Operations spend two days each week in "check rides" with delivery agents. Customer Service managers are required to do scheduled "check sits" with phone agents. These are not passive observations. The purpose is to help and to foster continuous improvement. These "rides" and "sits" are not predicated on existing problems but rather a proactive position predicated on "an ounce of prevention."

Share expectations and goals.

Dominant steps in the Coaching Model: Step 2, Define the Topic and Need. The majority of time is spent understanding what has been done, what is in progress, and what is going to happen. Both parties need to share the same expectations or goals for each of these areas. This status check is, however, only part of the discussion. The other part allows both parties to focus on concerns or issues that may only be minor but need attention. This is an excellent opportunity to discuss those areas that might be potential problems or to consider needed changes in the future direction of the work. Think of this as tweaking or fine tuning. It is gentle coaching that involves helping make those mid-course corrections that, if ignored, could become major issues at a later time. Step 3, Establish Impact, only becomes relevant if there is resistance to these mid-course corrections. Otherwise, it is appropriate to jump to Step 4, Initiate a Plan, without discussing Step 3. Since the tone of the discussion is review and improvement, not criticism or blame, both parties should be willing to jointly plan for maintaining present activities and making minor mid-course corrections. Step 5, Get A Commitment, is a natural conclusion of this joint review and planning process. Usually all that is needed is a confirmation that both parties are in agreement on how to proceed until the next reviewing discussion. *Fine tuning*

Additional efforts needed: Documentation of the agreed-to mid-course corrections is in order if these are complex and open to misinterpretation.

LEVEL 3: MENTORING

Your goal: To develop others' capabilities to succeed in a changing environment. Mentoring is the one level of coaching that deals with addition – to add a skill or competence. The focus is on learning. As Michael Hammer so succinctly states, "A successful career will no longer be about promotion. It will be about mastery."

When this is appropriate: Mentoring is helpful when changes occur, continual growth is required, competition demands more from you, you want to better meet customer needs, or the opportunity exists to be proactive in our development instead of waiting for others to make decisions about you and your future. The issue is not "if" change will occur but "how" you will adapt to it. Consider, more Americans... *Not if but how*

- *make computers than all forms of transport*
- *work in accounting firms than in the whole energy industry*
- *work in biotechnology than in making machine tools*

> • *work in the movie industry than the automotive*
> *industry*[3]

At the beginning of the 20th century there were no airline pilots and mechanics, medical technicians, fax machine workers, auto mechanics, or truck, bus, and taxi drivers.[4]

To not help others think about and plan for how tomorrow will be different from today is living in a state of denial. Coaching for only the "here-and-now" is managing, not leading. Most would agree that change occurred for them "with the help of others." A significant responsibility for the coach.

Dominant steps in the Coaching Model: Step 3, Establish Impact, and Step 6, Confronting Excuses and Resistance. The main stumbling block for people is fear, moving from their "comfort zone" to the unknown. The natural reaction is to rationalize why the "status quo" is acceptable. Skillfully helping others hold up the mirror and look at the intermediate and long term effects of maintaining the status quo is the key. The impact of not continually learning and growing needs to be made apparent, in contrast to the added value of growth and personal satisfaction. Change is a constant, and the most productive approach is to proactively help the other person see how to continue to grow and develop. This will require additional effort on the other person's part, and the coach needs to be prepared to think creatively about ways to facilitate this. The driving theme for the coach should be, "Let's figure out how we can make it happen and not dwell on how hard it will be or why it can't be done." Don't be overly concerned about what the plan will look like; in reality there will be a number of equally attractive options. The key is to create that internal sense of urgency and need in the other person and not to get stuck on the natural excuses and resistance to change. Then the rest of the steps in the coaching model will be easy.

Embrace and move forward

Additional efforts needed: Be prepared for the discussion by having considered all the possible ways that growth could be accomplished. Embracing and moving toward change are more important than a favored alternative. Be willing to let go and be creative.

LEVEL 4: CONFRONTING

Your goal: To address behaviors that are impeding effectiveness or personal satisfaction, or that don't measure up to core-position competencies.

When this is appropriate: Confronting is needed when things are not going right – the other person is in conflict with others, is not meeting minimum expectations, or is causing problems related to personal demeanor, style, or attitudes.

Dominant steps in the Coaching Model: This discussion is where all eight steps in the model come into play. However, Steps 1, Being Supportive; 2, Define the Topic and Needs; and, 3, Establish Impact, are where the majority of time will be spent. Projecting a sincere concern and willingness to help the other person achieve his or her goals, helping both parties better understand how and when the current behavior(s) are creating the problem, looking at how the current behavior is negatively impacting or impeding the individual from achieving personal goals as well as the goals of the team – these are the keys to helping this person both come to grips with the problem and establish the foundation for developing action plans to remedy the situation.

Additional efforts needed: The coach needs to document the process both as a tangible record of the conversation and a way of making sure that both parties agree on the needed changes and new directions.

Document changes and new directions

LEVEL 5: CHOOSING

Your goal: To clarify your intentions, choices, and options when things are not working out. It is important to be realistic with one another, with the recognition that any future relationship is contingent upon a decision and signs from the other person.

When this is appropriate: This level is needed under the following circumstances: The other person is unwilling or unable to change. After numerous unsuccessful Level-4 conversations, you're frustrated and doubt if you can be a source of help. There appears to be a mismatch.

A sales office in a remote location needed a full-time administrative assistant for continuity in the absence of the sales person. In the initial interview the sales person made it clear that if the applicant needed "social interaction with others," this position would not meet that criteria. A person was selected, and after one year of employment the sales person noted an increasing trend of personal calls and personal visits from various family members. Having spent sufficient time on the previous levels, three Level-4 discussions were held, each ending with a commitment to handle all personal and family business during a set lunch hour or after work. Two weeks after the last level-4 discussion, the sales person had to be in the office and answered most of the phone calls. On two successive days, 15 and 18 personal calls from friends or family members were made to the administrative assistant. Clearly the situation had not changed and appeared to be getting worse. With a great deal of frustration, the sales person scheduled a Level-5 coaching discussion. After a review of past discussions, the frustration with progress, and the current behavior, the sales person concluded with these statements, "All signs indicate that you need a job which allows you more social interaction. This job does not provide those opportunities, and this appears to be very frustrating for you. My suggestion is that you take tomorrow off, with pay, and think about what you want to do. If you want to stay here, the personal calls and visits have to be eliminated. If this job does not provide the kind of social interaction you need, then you will need to find another job. At this juncture these are the only two choices I see. When you return I need your decision on what would be best for you and what you want to do."

Move forward   From personal experience, being able to say, "I've done all that I can. It's time to let it go; the ball's in your court" to yourself and the other person is a very calming end to a frustrating and emotionally trying period of time. When you've done all you can, giving up is freedom, not failure. Both you and the other person are free to get on with life without guilt. You have recognized the mismatch, tried to help, achieved no progress and decided that the best solution is to disengage. Or the other person makes a commitment to get involved in working with you to effect the needed changes.

Dominant steps in the Coaching Model: A clear statement about your frustrations and willingness to give up can both establish the seriousness of this discussion and offer the other person the choice to engage in a productive alternative that may encourage you to continue working with him or her. "In my mind I have done what I thought would help, and I see little progress. I am at a loss. I feel stuck. Do you have any ideas? If not, we need to focus on what has happened in our previous discussions and what the steps are for us after today."

Start with your conclusions about Step 8; then review what has been discussed in previous meetings in Steps 2, 3, and 4. This is the time for a direct and honest assessment of the inability or unwillingness to change. With this in mind the coach has an obligation to be clear about Step 7, Clarify the Consequences, in terms of outcomes that are inevitable after this discussion and to leave, at the other person's discretion, a pathway of hope. You are not there to punish or put the other person down, just to clarify the available options and conclusions. "I have tried, to no avail, to help you achieve the expectations for your position; as a result, these are the consequences of the course of action you have chosen to pursue. . . .For it to be different would require that you work with me on the needed changes. My suggestion is that you think about this for a day; then you tell me what you want to do". *Clarify options*

Additional efforts needed: This discussion will occur in a minority of cases during your career as a coach. When it does, the key is to be prepared. Make sure all previous discussions have been documented in detail and that the other person is aware of these documents. The second area of preparation is to know the next steps required by your organization if termination, a time off without pay to think about the decision, or other alternatives are appropriate.

DEEPER CAUSES OF COACHING FAILURES

Many coaching failures are attributed to the lack of time, the coach's conflicting priorities, or the attitude and reputation of the other person. We think in some cases it goes deeper than this: the coach hasn't gone through the levels, hasn't paid his or her dues. As the following example illustrates, if you ignore Levels 1-3 coaching, it is easy to let your emotions take you to an immediate Level-4 or Level-5 coaching discussion.

"Hi Conrad, you wanted to see me?"

"Yes, Alice, there's some bad news, so I will get right to it – I am afraid that you are seen as ineffective on the projects you have worked on and the decision has been made to reassign you to a less demanding position."

"How can that be? This is really a shock. None of my

clients ever complained! This sounds fishy and I will have to see what legal recourse I have."

What happened? Alice has spent fifteen years with this organization progressing through the Engineering Department to the level of lead project engineer. Although more of an introvert, she is confident, considerate, and thoughtful. However there has been some feedback from the Marketing Department on the efficiency and speed with which projects have been completed: "The engineers weren't working hard or fast enough to complete the redesign efforts for the customers." Conrad, the Director of Engineering, served as an insulator, protecting the engineers from the wrath of the Marketing Department. Thus the engineers did not fully understanding the magnitude or seriousness of the issue or how much visibility this issue was getting during the Management Committee meetings.

Conrad felt the feedback from Marketing was both critical and degrading; he ignored, then "colored" the feedback given to Alice. With the best intentions, Conrad tried to protect and deflect some of the harsh criticism of Alice's performance. He had both fallen short of or neglected his Level-2 coaching responsibilities and was responsible for collusion. An honest discussion and assessment of the feedback from Marketing should have occurred months before this final discussion. In the Management Committee meetings Alice became branded as ineffective, losing respect and having her credibility damaged. The issue became bigger than Alice or Conrad, resulting in the eventual reassignment. Unfortunately, for Alice it was too late for coaching.

Go through all five levels
Too many Level-5 discussions are a result of the coach not going through the other four levels. The blame is easily shifted to others when, in fact, it rests squarely on the coach's shoulders. Plan for and take the time to coach those you work with on Levels 1-4. Jumping to Level 5 is not coaching; it is just cutting your losses.

[1]Sports Illustrated, October 2, 1995

[2]Fortune, October 14, 1996, "This Tough Guy Wants To Give You A Hug"

[3]Nuala Beck, *Shifting Gears: Thriving In The New Economy*

[4]Michael Cox and Richard Alm, "The Churn: The Paradox of Progress," Federal Reserve Bank of Dallas 1992 Annual Report

5

Versatile Coaching and the Myers-Briggs Type Indicator

Think about people with whom you find it particularly frustrating to communicate. You seem to be on two different wavelengths. They are hard to understand or predict. When you want to be specific, they want to talk big picture, or when you want to speculate on possibilities, they want to be sensible, or when you want to be brief and logical, they want to look at all the implications, discover all the missing details – the differences go on and on. To paraphrase a popular book title, they seem to be from Venus while you are from Mars. It is fashionable to say that these differences are to be valued, which may be true. But these interactions are often frustrating, which results in communication failure or, worse yet, no communication at all. It is just too painful when these extreme differences exist. In order to value these differences, we need to understand them and to let them guide how we work and communicate.

It is a given that no two people are alike. When asked what to do if a person has trouble grasping the impact of the situation or can't seem to figure out what to do during a coaching discussion, the natural response is "it depends." The great unknown variable is who the other person is. What is known about the other person's values, goals, and preferences will help determine which approach will be most productive. The good salesperson, speaker, or leader is sensitive to who their client, audience, or followers are. So too, effective coaches must be versatile in how they approach and interact with different people. With our own employees we know intuitively, on a case-by-case basis, what approach will

No two people are alike.

be more effective with Mary, Jonathan, or Chris. Yet, is there any way of thinking about these differences between people in a more systematic and general way? A way that has direct implications for communicating with others more effectively?

Differences exist

Various approaches are available to assess and identify the differences that exist between people. A widely used tool for understanding differences between people is the *Myers-Briggs Type Indicator* (MBTI)[1], based on the work of psychiatrist C. G. Jung. This is a commonly used instrument for greater self-awareness, and it serves as a window for seeing others more clearly. Part of understanding and accepting others' differences is recognizing your own Myers-Briggs preferences. The questionnaire is easy to complete, and the only requirement is that you obtain it from an MBTI-certified person. Or, by pointing your computer's search utility to MBTI and selecting the appropriate home page, you can take the Keirsey Temperament version and have it scored online. Rather than delve deeply into all aspects of the MBTI, we will focus on those critical differences between people that have implications for coaching discussions.

Coaching, in its simplest form, is the process of helping others accurately assess their current situation and decide what changes to implement. In this context, the MBTI is particularly useful. When discussions are focused on influencing, explaining, or trying to understand, people have different preferences for perceiving, which includes the process of becoming aware of things, people, occurrences, ideas, and judging, which includes the process of coming to conclusions and making decisions about what has been perceived. If people differ on these two basic preferences, then it follows that they will also differ in their reactions, values, motivations, skills, and interests.

TWO WAYS OF PERCEIVING OR TAKING IN DATA

Sensors (S) (75% of the pop.)	*Intuitives (N)* (25% of the pop.)
Are factual, concrete	Look at the global scheme, the world of possibilities
Want to be tangible and specific	Focus on abstraction, dreams, the future
Reach conclusions step by step	Reach conclusions quickly
Use the 5 senses	Use the 6th sense
Espouse "If it ain't broke don't fix it."	Live in anticipation
Are sensible, here and now	Prefer metaphors and vivid imagery, value hunches

Key words

Sensors (S) (75% of the pop.)	*Intuitives (N)* (25% of the pop.)
Realistic, actual, facts, practical, sensible Advocate "Seeing is believing"	Speculative, vision of the future, ingenious, imaginative

Sensor as *Described by Intuitive*	*Intuitive as* *Described by Sensor*
Plodding, exasperatingly slow to see possibilities	Impractical, unrealistic, skips from one activity to the next, appears to be flighty, absent-minded

If asked the question, "How do I drive from Chicago to St. Louis?" the responses of the Sensor and the Intuitive will differ dramatically:

Sensor: From downtown Chicago, get on I44 South. At the intersection of I55, go west, heading toward Joliet. Stay on I55 for 135 miles, then take the by-pass around Bloomington. Sixty-two miles later is Springfield, the state capital. Also take the by-pass around that city. Continue south for 90 miles to the town of East St. Louis, etc., etc., etc.

Intuitive: Head south on I55 and you'll run into it – you can't miss it.

TWO WAYS OF JUDGING OR MAKING DECISIONS
(the only preference with a gender bias)

Thinkers (T) (50% of the pop.) (66% males)	*Feelers (F)* (50% of the pop.) (66% females)
Are logical and orderly	Appeal to emotions
Are objective and impersonal	Are people oriented, respond to others' feelings
List the costs and benefits	Show how decision supports personal goals
Are analytically oriented	Are subjectively oriented
Reason from cause to effect	Want door left open
Use rules to govern choices	Make emotion-laden decisions

Key words:

Thinkers (T) (50% of the pop.)	*Feelers (F)* (50% of the pop.)
Objective, principles, policy, law, criteria, firmness, justice, standards, critical analysis	Subjective, values, extenuating circumstances, intimacy, persuasion, humane, harmony, sympathy, devotion

Thinkers as Described by Feeler	Feelers as Described by Thinker
Heartless, ice in their veins, remote, lacking the milk of human kindness	Too soft hearted, unable to take a stand, too emotional, illogical fuzzy thinkers, wear their heart on their sleeve

The motivation for taking a break during a meeting reveals differences between a Thinker and a Feeler:

Thinker: We've covered the first half of the agenda, it makes sense, to take a break.

Feeler: We've worked hard, and we all seem to be exhausted, so we deserve to take a break.

GENERAL OBSERVATIONS ABOUT THE PREFERENCES FOR PERCEIVING AND JUDGING

These preferences are not either/or, but vary in degree. In the case of handedness, a preference for using the left hand does not preclude the use of the right hand. Similarly, just because a person prefers to understand things intuitively doesn't exclude the use of the senses; and a preference to make decisions rationally and logically doesn't mean a person lacks strong feelings.

MBTI is only one way to view human personality. Many other attitudes combine to make people who they are, gender, ethnicity, values, age, and socioeconomic factors. Characterizing people as one of these four types does not capture the essence of their humanity and can lead to false assumptions.

In addition to Sensor-Intuitive and Thinker-Feeler, there are two other sets of preferences: Extraversion[2]-Introversion, and Judgment-Perception. These are not discussed because they have less significance for coaching and communication with others.

Preferences have various strengths

The reader should be cognizant that preferences have various strengths. We have concentrated on the extremes – highest preference – to make the differences vivid. However, these differences would not be as pronounced if the person had only a slightly stronger preference for Sensing over Intuiting or for Thinking over Feeling. Everything is relative; there are no absolutes.

The opposites actually need their counterparts to complement each other in any joint undertaking. The clearest vision of the future may come from an Intuitive, the most practical realism from a Sensor, the most incisive analysis from a Thinker, and the most skillful handling of people from a Feeler. Success in any endeavor demands a variety of types. Disagreements are constructive and not irritating when Joyce recognizes that Donna cannot be expected to agree. Donna is not being willfully contrary; she is simply expressing her preference. Neither is right or wrong, better or best; they are just different. Good coaches have tolerance and an understanding of these differences. The list below shows some of the specific ways opposites can be useful[3]:

Intuitives Need Sensing Types:	*Sensing Types Need Intuitives:*
To bring up pertinent facts	To bring up new possibilities
To apply experience to problems	To supply ingenuity to problems
To have patience	To have enthusiasm
To keep track of essential details	To watch for new essentials
To face difficulties with realism	To tackle difficulties with zest

Feeling Types Need Thinkers:	*Thinkers Need Feeling Types:*
To analyze	To persuade
To organize	To conciliate
To find the flaws in logic in advance	To forecast how others will feel
To hold consistently to a policy	To teach, to sell
To stand firm against opposition	To appreciate the thinker

THE IMPLICATIONS OF THE MBTI FOR COACHING?

First, if Step One, Support, is awkward or seems like swimming upstream you are likely to be a Sensor/Thinker who likes things rational and logical. The vast majority of managers we work with appear to be Sensor/Thinkers. If this is true, more patience and acceptance of the other three types will be required. Sensor/Thinkers also have to work harder during the "softer" feeling times in coaching conversations with others.

Second, Step One is the core of effective coaching, composing 50% of the total time, which speaks to the value of MBTI. Acceptance of the individual, suspension of judgment, and a sincere willingness to be coached yourself create a climate in which constructive dialogue can occur. Many of the managers we work with struggle to put their agenda on the back burner in order to listen and hear the other person.

Step One is the core

Peter Senge calls this the difference between advocacy and inquiry. Regardless of your or the other person's MBTI, inquiry is supportive behavior, like a thread that should weave through the entire conversation.

COACHING THE SENSOR/FEELER

A Sympathetic Friend and Advocate

These individuals are friendly and service oriented. They trust their feelings and make decisions with personal warmth, weighing how much things matter to themselves and others. They are sensitive to others' reactions and feelings, value personal loyalty, and are gracious, easy-going, and low keyed, with an accepting manner.

Step One: Be Supportive

The Sensor/Feeler seeks support and encouragement more than the other three types. This individual's focus is on results that positively impact people. The Sensor/Feeler will be more responsive if treated in a sensitive manner; it is especially important to convey an attitude of respect and empathy. Avoid criticism or the appearance of criticism of other team members in an open forum (we don't know why the coach would do this anyway).

Step Two: Define the Topic and Needs

The most effective approach is to be straightforward with facts and details. The Sensor/Feeler lives in the present, here and now. If the topic to be addressed involves practical issues within a context of relationships, you can anticipate a receptive individual. However, if the topic involves future results or if the benefits are neither obvious nor explicit, you can expect resistance and excuses. If you encounter resistance, the best approach is to appeal to the Sensor/Feeler's bias for a friendly and service-oriented environment and explain how this issue adversely impacts these areas.

Step Three: Establish Impact

Establishing impact is best accomplished by engaging in a discussion about how the issue is affecting either the individual themselves or those with whom the individual must interact. You can illustrate the personal impact of the behavior and its effect on others. This individual's alliance is with people and trusts his/her "gut feeling" about the impact of individual behavior on relationships. The more the coach can set the discussion in a personal context, the better. An appeal to ambitions or needs for achievement will fall on deaf ears.

Step Four: Initiate a Plan

Plans that involve the human element and reality-based outcomes are this individual's forte, as opposed to plans that are impersonal and/or abstract. As an illustration, the Sensor/Feeler would like assignments that include evaluating worker roles and responsibilities, assessing skills and related developmental needs, or seeing to it that no one individual is having to do an unfair share of the work. This individual would be uncomfortable dealing with new and untested procedures.

Step Five: Get a Commitment

You need to beware of shallow or vacillating commitments, because in an attempt to please others, the Sensor/Feeler may hedge and waffle. If the individual is expected to take a stand that will affect and possibly offend others, it may be helpful if you, as the coach, are present to provide support and encouragement. The desire to not offend others includes you and, therefore, the Sensor/Feeler may tell you what he/she thinks you want to hear. It is important that you convey to this individual that he/she should be candid with you regarding his/her level of commitment.

Step Six: Confront Excuses and Resistance

The Sensor/Feeler values the needs of the individual more than the needs of society. This bias, when combined with the fact that no one person's situation or experience is identical to another's, makes it easy and natural for this individual to think of exceptions, hence resistance and excuses. As a coach, your challenge will be to recognize the possible validity of the expressed exception, while at the same time encouraging this individual to think about broader implications. If those implications can be linked to something other than operational efficiencies, so much the better. Don't be surprised by displays of emotions. This individual is often fighting a noble fight…defending the rights and needs of others.

Step Seven: Clarify Consequences, Don't Punish

The benefits should be explicitly stated not just implied. This individual prefers the immediate, or here and now, and may not readily anticipate future or long-term consequences. You will want to relate your view of how things will look, and what relationships will be like after a plan is successfully implemented.

Step Eight: Don't Give Up

This individual is driven by the practical realities of day-to-day relationships, a natural segue to Step Eight. Checking in on progress and unmet needs will appeal to this individual's emphasis on and concern for others.

COACHING THE SENSOR/THINKER
"Just the facts ma'am, just the facts"

This famous line by Sergeant Friday of Dragnet best sums up this person's interest in the realities of a given situation. Reality is what can be observed, collected, and verified directly by the senses – by seeing, hearing, touching, etc. After observation, decisions are made by logical analysis, using a step-by-step process of reasoning from cause to effect, from premise to conclusion.

Step One: Be Supportive

This person takes pride in being practical and sensible. You can be supportive by recognizing that he/she likes to manage costs and schedules using statistics, graphs, and charts. This individual likes to solve problems immediately, rather than procrastinating. These preferences have definite value to the organization, department, and team.

Step Two: Define the Topic and Needs

The best approach is to be straightforward with facts and details and to get to the point quickly, because this individual finds small talk extraneous. A good lead in might be, "In a nutshell, here is how I see the situation. . ." If the topic to be addressed involves measurable results supported by statistics and a need for short-term problem solving, you should confront little or no resistance. However, if the topic involves personal or personnel-related matters, speculation, or long-term problem solving, you are likely to face excuses and resistance. If you encounter resistance, you can appeal to this individual's bias towards efficiency and stability by demonstrating the disruptive effect of the current behavior.

Step Three: Establish Impact

You can demonstrate how the current behavior affects the practical here and now, e.g., time and money. A meaningful conversation about cost-to-benefit ratios can create internal motivation. You are unlikely to make a difference with this person unless the topic relates directly and practically to the work or task at hand. Introspection, brainstorming, and hypothesizing will be consciously avoided.

Step Four: Initiate a Plan

This step in the coaching process is relatively easy. Detailed, time-focused activity is a strength of the Sensor/Thinker, so it's best to stay out of the way and let him/her do it. This individual is self-regulating and needs minimal supervision. However, if the topic being addressed involves issues which are, in the Sensor/Thinker's view, abstract, esoteric, theoretical, and hence irrelevant, then you will have to take a more active role in mapping out an action plan.

Step Five: Get a Commitment

Committing to a plan should not be a problem. The more practical the plan, the better. If you detect hesitation or reservation, the strategy should be to retrace your previous "steps" to identify ambiguity associated with the action plan and/or the individual's suspicion of the facts or details. If the plan is aimed at an issue that is less than concrete, the Sensor/Thinker will be anxious about measuring the desired outcome; he/she will want the coach to help answer the question, "How will I know when the plan is accomplished?" Creating measurable, observable milestones will assist in eliciting a commitment.

Step Six: Confront Excuses and Resistance

The extent to which you encounter excuses and resistance

will depend on the degree to which the topic/need and supporting evidence are specific, factual, and logical. You shouldn't be surprised or become defensive if this person challenges your observations or assumptions and asks for proof. It is helpful to have your facts and figures close by, rather than trying to "wing it." Notwithstanding, this individual's strong preference for logical data-driven decisions, when compared to other preference combinations, the Sensor/Thinker contributes a high level of loyalty to the organization and is willing to subjugate personal needs to those in authority. This might explain why the Sensor/Thinker is often found in military and industrial settings.

Step Seven: Clarify Consequences, Don't Punish

The Sensor/Thinker tends not to look too far beyond the immediate here and now. Anticipating longer term consequences without your assistance will be difficult. If it is appropriate to clarify consequences, you can help this individual to see the practical benefits, albeit in the future. This is especially important if the plan requires a stretch beyond the Sensor/Feeler's comfort zone.

Step Eight: Don't Give Up

Driven by measurable results this individual likes to be responsible and accountable and would find regularly scheduled follow-up meetings beneficial. These provide the coach with the opportunity for ongoing support in the form of constructive and timely feedback, as well as recognition of the individual's accomplishments.

COACHING THE INTUITIVE/FEELER
Idealistic Do Gooder

This person takes pride in being personal and concerned about the feelings of others. He/she eats, sleeps, thinks, breathes and loves people. The idealist of life, he/she is attracted by new projects, things that have not happened yet but might be made to happen, new truths that are not yet known but might be found out, or above all, new possibilities for people. Your discussions with this individual will be more conversational. This person is very tender minded and appreciates an indirect approach that allows self-discovery and independently reaching conclusions. These conversations have the potential of being more emotional than the other three.

Step One: Be Supportive

The Intuitive/Feeler's strong desire to help others makes him/her likable and easy to support. This individual has a phenomenal capacity to work with people and draw out their best. You will want to affirm this valuable contribution. In response to this individual's tendency to talk about ideals, you should take time to listen with genuine interest. You need not be too concerned with practicality or achievability, as many changes or discoveries would never have happened without a dream.

Step Two: Define the Topic and Needs

This individual will justify behavior in terms of his/her fellow man. The most important thing is to be in harmony with others. The Intuitive/Feeler prefers higher level issues, especially as they relate to individuals If the topic of discussion is detailed or factual in nature, you will want to create a context in which harmony, innovation, or personal growth are also at stake. This individual likes to look at the forest not the trees. As a coach you may have to start with a discussion of the forest and then pick out a specific tree as part of this larger picture.

Step Three: Establish Impact

Your objective will be to demonstrate how this topic or need, if addressed, will enhance relationships, not of particular individuals but rather for the group as whole. An extreme example of an Intuitive/Feeler is the college instructor who said, "I love and value mankind, it's individuals I can't stand." Issues of morale and making the most of human potential are the Intuitive/Feeler's drivers. Criticism should be handled delicately since it may be personalized and result in needless hurt feelings. Attempting to get this individual's attention by referring to costs, schedules, documentation, paperwork, hierarchies, and the like will be an uphill battle. The Intuitive/Feeler is receptive to discussions that address organizational core values; concern is focused on being a member of an organization that stands for something, one that takes the high road. A successful strategy is to link the issue or topic to a higher purpose or calling, especially in relation to mankind.

Step Four: Initiate a Plan

For the Intuitive/Feeler, the detailed nature of the planning process may prove uncomfortable. In the words of a well known song, these are "people who need people," and the Intuitive/Feeler would probably benefit from collaborating with you in the planning process. Such demonstrated support is precisely the approach this individual would take in a coaching situation and therefore would be well received. This individual is a natural team builder and leader, bringing out the best in others. If the topic or problem being addressed involves issues that either ignore or are detrimental to the well-being of others, the Intuitive/Feeler is likely to resist.

Step Five: Get a Commitment

If the plan is seen as adversely affecting others, the Intuitive/Feeler's preference for harmony and avoiding conflict may result in a shallow or qualified commitment. If the coach senses that this is the case, the best appeal is to this individual's strong propensity for personal integrity. Insist that he/she be forthright about any reservations. On the other hand, if the issue or actions to be taken enhance relationships, the coach can expect unqualified support and commitment. The Intuitive/Feeler will be an unabashed champion for the cause.

Step Six: Confront Excuses and Resistance

The level of excuses and resistance will depend on the nature of the topic or need. The Intuitive/Feeler avoid or resist issues that involve what is perceived as mundane and hence meaningless; e.g., budgets, schedules, hierarchies, and politics, as well as documentation and paperwork. This person's resistance may manifest itself in the form of passive aggression since confrontation is not a comfortable "style." As the coach, you may have to actively pursue this individual's concerns. They will eventually surface, better during the conversation than later.

Step Seven: Clarify Consequences, Don't Punish

Conversations about longer term or natural outcomes are easy for the Intuitive/Feeler. If the issue or topic being addressed is viewed as lacking value and meaning, the coach's challenge will be to convey why choosing to deny the need for action would be a mistake. The admonition in this step, "don't punish," is especially true when coaching the Intuitive/Feeler. This individual responds to encouragement and recognition. A heavy-handed approach will prove counterproductive. If the issue or topic is one that is consistent with this individual's view of the world, any discussion of consequences will be unnecessary Intuitive/Feelers will see it without having to be told, although he/she will likely appreciate being validated as insightful.

Step Eight: Don't Give Up

This final step in the coaching process will be relatively easy with the Intuitive/Feeler and is an excellent way of demonstrating the coach's ongoing commitment and support. Since this individual typically gives as well as needs strokes; is receptive to personalized, close contact; and prefers face-to-face dialogue, as a coach you will find follow-up sessions to be valued and needed. This individual needs empathetic support and encouragement. The appropriate treatment can make the difference between a highly energized member of your team and one whose efforts are channeled into mobilizing a revolution.

COACHING THE INTUITIVE/THINKER
"What If"

This person takes pride in being a visionary and conceptualizer. A bias for the big picture and for possibilities will result in discussions that are more speculative, exploratory, and "what if." The possibility of abstraction may require the coach to combine directness, to keep the discussion focused, with the time and space to explore.

Step One: Be Supportive

The Intuitive/Thinker likes to logically analyze things that are abstract and complex. As an employee or team member, this individual exhibits traits that others value. The coach's role is to listen with empathy and patience, being careful not to burst the bubble with here-and-now realities. This individual may resist more subjective and value-driven conversations. This will require patience, patience, patience – especially if the coach is a Sensor/Thinker.

Step Two: Define the Topic and Needs

This may prove challenging, depending on the nature of the topic or need. Excuses and resistance may emerge if the issue to be discussed involves details (trivia from the Intuitive's perspective) or human relations issues (irrelevant irrationality from the Thinker's perspective). The coach might appeal to this individual's sense of "possibilities" that such a discussion "might" or "could" have value. Or, the coach might first acknowledge how frustrating "details" and "people-problems" can be and solicit agreement that, like it or not, future possibilities are composed of current, here-and-now realities – the more intriguing and fascinating, the better. This step will be smoother if the coach can link the topic or need to the individual's bias for the future, the big picture, and objective data. Details may not be helpful, especially if they are based on hearsay or subjective interpretations. You are likely to be mentally challenged, so this is not the time to use improvised facts and figures but to be a credible source of information.

Step Three: Establish Impact

This step will be less difficult than the preceding steps. The Intuitive/Thinker is generally adept at grasping the meaning or implications of data by looking at the data in a linear, logical, and objective manner, devoid of emotions. What are the pros, what are the cons? If the coach encounters difficulty at this step, it is important to realize that principles, policy, and established criteria will bolster the argument. You can ask, "What's the right thing to do here"? Or, "Tell me what your standards for behavior would be in this situation." For this person, "Logic says it's right, and that's all that matters."

Step Four: Initiate a Plan

Planning requires active facilitation from the coach. The Intuitive/Thinker may generate imaginative solutions that are overly complex and a bit too theoretical. This individual will be inclined to overhaul an entire system rather than focus on the fire that is currently raging. The coach's challenge will be to help this individual remain focused on the immediate need and stay grounded while, at the same time, not smothering the "creative possibilities juices." This individual may underestimate the day-to-day effort required to make the future a reality. It may be helpful to request a written action plan to ensure that the two of you are clear about what is expected. Be patient; if time is not critical, it may be easier for the Intuitive/Thinker to develop a draft overview; with that in hand, the two of you can fill in the gaps. To this individual, the "devil is truly in the details." Your role, as coach, is to help "give the devil his due." Lastly, you need to be aware that solutions may not take into account the subjective realm of others' feelings. The individual will need to be encouraged to think through the impact on significant others.

Step Five: Get a Commitment

If the plan is logical, rational, and objective, this is a non-issue for the Intuitive/Thinker: "Lets do it." Listen for reservations or hesitation caused by this individual's "what if" tendencies and feelings that the plan has his/her hands tied. You need to be patient and, if possible to revisit the plan with the intent of making it less restrictive.

Step Six: Confront Excuses and Resistance

The coach's best bet with excuses and resistance is objective and logical analysis. The Intuitive/Thinker has a strong need for competency and as such will value the viewpoint of someone who is equally or more competent. Subjective opinions or points of view may be discounted and suspect. You may confront resistance if the topic, issue, or subject of the coaching discussion involves unproductive rules, regulations, or tradition.

Step Seven: Clarify Consequences, Don't Punish

This can be a motivation or catalyst for this individual, who likes systems or big-picture thinking. The coach might ask, "So tell me, what outcomes or consequences would you expect if this plan gets implemented?" The answer will provide the Intuitive/Thinker with his/her rationale or justification for moving forward; it will validate and confirm the coaching process.

Step Eight: Don't Give Up

"What if" scenarios and continuing to think about it can result in little or no action. Scheduled follow-up and review of the action plan, not to mention patience and continued support, will be both necessary and helpful.

THE ROLE OF THE COACH'S PREFERENCES

It might appear that we are suggesting you become a chameleon, changing with every person you interact with. Although versatile coaches have the ability to adjust their approaches to the people they are coaching, you also have the right to have your needs and preferences met. The best way of achieving this objective is to openly discuss your preferences with the other person. Coaching is a two-way street; it is not something you do to someone else. In the spirit of having an open discussion, the other person should be equally sensitive to your preferences. This will help each of you be clearer and more prepared for your differences and similarities during your discussions. We believe this is what is meant by the popular but often overused term, valuing differences. A first step in understanding and valuing differences is an open exchange about your preferences for perceiving and judging. Do the people you interact with and coach know your MBTI? Should they? We think so. And do you know theirs? A valuable follow-up to our Coaching Workshop has been to work with a team on how to use the MBTI to improve intra-team coaching conversations. Knowledge of individual preferences can enhance communication and facilitate the eight-step coaching process.

---

[1]©Consulting Psychology Press Inc. More than 2 million people took the MBTI in 1990.

[2]Misspelled intentionally for emphasis by the MBTI profession.

[3]Adapted from, Using the Myers-Briggs Type Indicator In Organizations (2nd edition) by Sandra Krebs Hirch. ©1991 by Consulting Psychologist Press, Inc.

6

Supporting Skills

THE FAULT FACTOR

"Everyone is responsible...and no one is to blame."

"Don't blame me" is the most popular game in corporate America these days. The safest path is to avoid ownership for mistakes or omissions. This pattern can be observed among managers at all levels, as well as among employees. It takes a lot of courage to admit mistakes, even if you have played only a contributing role. In truth, assigning fault or blame doesn't make a lot of difference if you agree with a forward-looking philosophy that advocates constructive action to deal with problems or to prevent them in the future. As mentioned earlier, employees clearly appreciate a leader who is willing to shoulder a fair share of the responsibility for problems. In fact, employees frequently attributed their cooperation and the success of coaching experiences to the leader's willingness to own up to his/her part of the problem and not to pretend to be a paragon of virtue. Some research suggests that leaders who hold employees primarily and personally responsible for concerns or problems are likely to come down excessively hard on employees and create a barrier in the relationship (often referred to as a disaffiliative effect). Unfortunately, some leaders fear that owning a share of the problem looks like a sign of weakness and that the employee will play this up and sidetrack the whole coaching discussion. If you have read this far, you know that you can handle this perceived threat and keep the discussion focused.

Forward looking philosophy

In reality, most problems and difficulties are caused by the interaction of many variables. Certainly, the employee is a key factor in situations that involve his/her job or assignment. The leader also plays a part, either directly or indirectly, and like the employee's, it is usually an inadvertent and unintended contribution. Sometimes leaders don't give clear assignments, define roles, or specify their expectations. Other contributing factors may include the organization's

*The contributors
to problems*

procedures, other units, and outside interference with the work such as government regulations, weather, equipment failure, communication breakdown, etc.

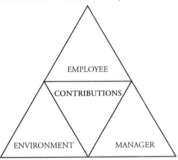

In most cases, many people and events contribute to the existence of problems and concerns. If you plan to launch a technical investigation, the most important challenge for you as leader is not to be trapped in the vicious and non-supportive fault-finding game. This simply moves your actions away from coaching. In some cases, a technical investigation and a detailed failure analysis may be appropriate. However, the coaching process is more concerned with establishing a course of action than with pathology. Please don't misunderstand. Analysis of cause can be an element of effective coaching, but it is not the main event. Focusing excessively on cause could be perceived and interpreted as a negative conversation and exchange by the employee.

*A better vision
of the future*

Remember, the main event is the creation of a better vision of the future. This means a clear direction, a jointly developed plan, and definite commitments to fix and prevent problems.

EMPLOYEES: ONE STEP AHEAD

"Don't shoot...we're on the same side."

Contrary to popular belief, the coaching session is not the beginning of the change process. Our studies and consulting indicate that, 90% of the time, employees already have a clue that a problem or challenge is on the horizon. Furthermore, some employees have already resolved to take action and correct an existing problem or prevent or minimize impending problems. This state of pre-existing readiness is called the employee's "own force" (self-motivation) for change. In a coaching session, the trick for the manager is not to let employees feel too threatened, exposed, or vulnerable when they sit down with you. If employees believe that they won't be tortured or tormented, they will begin to relax and share data and impressions. Employees will naturally feel some initial anxiety and be a bit defensive, even when they are in safe hands. The manager can achieve a lot of success if he/she can tap into, heighten, and acknowledge the employee's "own force" or self-recognition of the situation.

"Own force"

Some leaders believe that the coaching session will help the employee who has perceptual blind spots by establishing the fact that a problem exists. However, the real challenge is to eliminate blind spots regarding the problem's impact and consequences of future action.

A common omission of leaders, while conducting a coaching discussion, is acknowledging and giving employees credit for their awareness of the problem or concern voluntary cooperation, and self-recognition of the needed change. After gathering research data on the coaching process from both leaders and employees, we saw a fascinating pattern emerge. Leaders typically attributed their past coaching success to their own skillful orchestration of the coaching discussion. Employees, on the other hand, frequently attributed coaching success to their self-motivated effort to respond to change. Failure to understand that both the leader and employee play key parts in the coaching process can lead to serious complications.

Give employees credit

From our experience, employees generally don't transmit graphic or extravagant verbal or nonverbal signs that they are attuned to the leader's line of thought and recognize that change is needed. It is as though the employee doesn't want to let on that the manager has a very good point which deserves serious consideration. That manager needs to be very alert and prepared to recognize and acknowledge a subtle yet positive shift of direction or recognition from the employee. The ability to put this into words is critical. For instance, if the employee says, "I guess I would be willing to give that a try," the leader could either assume that the

Managers need to be alert to subtle cues

employee is still not fully committed or that this represents some positive movement and respond by saying, "I am glad you are willing to try. It is important to be sure that you want to go ahead with this plan."

The objective of this procedure is to support the employee's internal willingness or motivation to act constructively in the future. If the supervisor can recognize and reinforce the employee's "own force," then the ease and speed of the change will increase. One gets a dramatic sense of this phenomenon when listening carefully to employee accounts of previous coaching experiences. The following are word-for-word quotations from employees interviewed:

Quotations from employees

> "I could see the nature of my supervisor's concern. I felt really bad about it. When these problems occur they have a tremendous impact on our work."

> "Every error that is created results in an error for the company in terms of overpayments or underpayments."

> "I wanted to fix it as fast as my supervisor did. I knew that fixing this now would help me in the future."

> "My leader has a valid point. I probably had been wrong."

> "I was impatient. I wanted to correct it. If he had let this slide, it would have been a big problem later on."

Employees value expressions of appreciation in exchange for their support. If the leader doesn't acknowledge the employee's "own force" and treats the employee as though there were none, the employee may interpret the leader's actions as unnecessarily punitive or a put-down. This may result from the leader overworking the issue or covering old ground from the employee's point of view. The leader simply needs to make sure that the employee's awareness is accurate and that the level of readiness is high enough, and then guide the employee into an action plan.

The goal in all of this is to let employees feel like a part of the team, to recognize that employees have accurately detected the same concern or issue as the leader, and then to move the coaching process into the action plan. The bottom line is this: be prepared to give employees some credit, look for the subtle signs that they are beginning to respond, and express your appreciation for their support and cooperation.

STYLE – "TO CONTROL OR NOT TO CONTROL"

Communication style can be a confusing term. In coaching situations, it is simply the level of intensity exhibited by the leader, or the amount the leader "presses," during each of the coaching steps. We contend that leaders can choose to be very direct or very indirect in pointing out the opportunities, concerns, plans, consequences, etc., to the employee.

The amount of press

Our findings indicate that in routine coaching situations (not emergencies), the best style for starting the coaching session is one that is less direct – more probing, questioning, and data gathering in nature. Any change in the leader's style should be justifiable. For example, if the employee fails to respond to the manager's flexibility and patience, the leader may use more direction and intensity to insure movement and progress toward the desired change and to complete the coaching steps. However, the risk is that moving up the intensity scale too fast may create unnecessary employee alienation and resentment.

Employees report that their cooperation and motivation to change or improve a situation are largely based on their ability to see the issue, realize its impact, and formulate new actions and plans without heavy or excessive control or direction from a leader. So a leader who is patient and backs away from the heavy control or press may avoid offending the employee and enable this natural ability within employees to operate.

If the employee doesn't initially respond to a low-press style, the manager can test out a more direct and controlling style to complete the coaching cycle. A change in style works best when a leader moves in a direction from lower to higher intensity or control. It is more painful, especially for the employee, to move from a high-press or "pushing" style back to a low-press or "pulling" style. The analogy can be made to running over the employee with a "Mack truck" and then rushing in to rescue the employee when you find out it did-

It's hard to move back to less direct

n't take that much punch! It is hard to pick employees up, dust them off, apologize, and ask for their support after they have been hammered.

| LOW PRESS | HIGH PRESS |
| STARTING RANGE | |

⟶ *preferred direction of movement in the communication process*

It's okay to use high press

A lot of leaders ask us if it is okay to get tough with employees. We don't mind giving out permission slips to get tough if leaders have tried to resolve the issue using good-faith attempts to be supportive, patient, and honest. Frankly, some employees need direction and prescriptions. The key is not to handle all employees like that. The astute leader will know when to back off and create some psychological space or operating room for the employee and when it becomes necessary to press. You will probably need to vary your style between employees at different times and for different steps in the coaching model. By all means, if circumstances outside of your control are dictating the course of action, let the employees know this so your actions and intentions are not misinterpreted as aggressiveness; e.g., "Our timetable is short, so this has to be done this way or we're sunk." Just let them know that you want to work with them, utilize their abilities, and recognize their maturity and skill, when possible.

"The inclination to aggression... constitutes the greatest impediment to civilization."
– Sigmund Freud

BEING DESCRIPTIVE: ATTACK THE CONCERN, NOT THE PERSON

S.D.N. Specific Descriptive Non-Punishing

The Eight Steps can seem very confrontive to the employee, so you walk a tightrope at times and run the risk of sounding nonsupportive. Good coaching requires the leader to exchange views and perceptions about the problem at hand or the opportunities available to the employee. The key to effectively managing and presenting information to the employee is "SDN" or Specific, Descriptive, and Non-Punishing. The art of being specific and descriptive is deceptively simple: the leader merely names and describes the employee's actions. For instance, if the employee is coming to work late, you can say, "I have noticed that you are checking in at 8:20." Or if the employee turns in a report late you can say, "I noticed that you turned in the report on the 10th rather than the 5th." The next step requires patience and silence. You just "hit the ball" into the employee's court. Let the employee respond, excuse, justify, or rationalize (all of which are normal and should even be expected; be prepared to tolerate and accommodate those expressions with empathy and without giving up on future solutions or corrective changes). By allowing the employee to express some views, you are giving him/her a chance to be heard, and you are demonstrating your willingness to interact and listen (key supportive skills). If the employee asks you whether the behavior you described is a problem, simply say "yes." That is enough. Then let the employee pursue his/her thoughts, vent, or explain further.

Unfortunately, some leaders attack the person in a more forceful and nonsupportive fashion. The leader sounds more punitive when he/she says, "You are always late for work" or "Your report is late again, as usual." The motives behind these types of remarks are usually punishment, embarrassment, or getting even. The hope is that this aggressive approach will force the employee to change. Often the leader is acting out of highly charged emotions, anger, and frustration. These too are normal for leaders, but counterproductive. They can best be handled with a little preparation time and by thinking descriptively about the behavior.

How attack sounds

The "SDN" approach, on the other hand, is born out of the need to be fair, clear, and as objective as possible with the employee. Even with your best efforts, the employee may misinterpret your motives. If that seems to be happening, simply say that your intent is to be clear and not to blame, accuse, or put the employee down. If you can learn to describe actions and performance like an engineer would describe a valve (facts, dimensions, specifications, etc.), without injecting emotionally charged innuendoes, putdowns, or biased hints, you will create a starting point for the coaching session that will be constructive and less threatening to the employee.

Fair, clear, objective

PUTTING YOUR EXPECTATIONS TO WORK

Webster defines "boss" as one who exercises control or authority, one who directs or supervises workers.

A common notion is that leaders are the bosses and have the power and authority to make things happen with employees. Power can easily be intentionally or unintentionally abused or misinterpreted. We believe that leaders can effectively use indirect power and leverage and get better results than if they use aggressive, demanding, and controlling behavior. The art of using indirect leverage with employees lies in the power of clear expectations.

Indirect leverage lies in clear expectations.

Employees and leaders have fascinated us by their incessant references to the role that clear leader expectations (goals) played in facilitating change in the employee's performance and how these aided the coaching process. In fact, from the data we gathered from leaders, employees, and real coaching discussions, expectations were probably the most dominant of the initiation or problem-solving behaviors.

Leaders had these comments in reference to expectations:

Examples

> *"I told him it was essential that the project be completed by the deadline."*

> *"I told her I didn't want her to quit, and I needed her to be a team player."*

> *"I said we must honor established organizational procedures."*

> *"I explained to him that I needed to go over the reports before they were presented."*

> *"I want accurate reports."*

> *"I told her that it was unacceptable to not keep me informed when she was in trouble."*

Employees had this to say:

> *"She said she needed everyone's full cooperation."*

> *"He said failures like this should never happen again."*

> *"My manager made it clear that if I had questions, I should ask."*

> *"She said in this organization, you have to be cost effective and still be considerate of customers."*

> *"He told me to slow down and be more analytical."*

A leader simply needs to state what he/she wants from the employee, listen to the employee's response, and then seek agreement and commitment to the goals and expectations. The purpose of this procedure is to enable the employee to say to anyone, "I know what my job is in this situation." We have found that leaders understate and underrate the power of expectations when, in fact, they should be prepared to state and restate expectations so the employee can gain a clear vision of the leader's direction. This process is much like a contracting process in which wants and offers are exchanged.

State what you want

It is tempting and time efficient for leaders to "bark out" orders and demands based on the authority and power of their positions. However, our data suggests that leaders simply need to clarify the end objectives and then give the employee an opportunity to develop and contribute by generating the means of achieving the ends. Expectations then take on the role of an employee "self-monitoring" mechanism, especially when the expectations are clear, understood, and accepted. Much evidence suggests that the expectations and goals should be highly challenging in order to achieve the best results. Once the goals are in place, leaders can simply call attention to and keep the employee focused on them. Expectations allow the employee to do more self managing and require less "bossing" by the leaders. Employees can do more self-evaluation, thus allowing the leaders to do less judging and criticizing.

More "self management," less "bossing"

QUESTIONS AND SILENCE

"Silence is the most underutilized communication tool!"

This problem emerges over and over again: managers try to power their way through a difficult coaching situation with a monologue or lecture to the employee. It is appropriate for a leader to let the employee know what he/she is thinking and to keep the employee on track, but we also believe that questions and measured silence are underutilized techniques. For instance, a leader may want to tell the employee about the consequences of closing a large sale: "You know, Joan, that this sale means you will earn an extra $1,500 bonus." The other available option for the leader to make the same point is to encourage the employee to think

"Don't talk unless you can improve the silence."
– Vermont Proverb

and articulate by asking questions: "Joan, how much bonus will this sale generate for you?" Even if the employee requires a little time to respond, a little silence allows the impact of your point to sink in. In fact, it is probably good if Joan has to figure out (with a pencil and paper) that this sale means a great deal to her. Don't be afraid to use rhetorical or simplistic questions on occasion. For example, "What effect do you think this sale will have on your sales goal?" The point is simply this: questions and silence encourage the employee to

Allow the employee to think and discover

think and concentrate instead of just passively listening to you talk. This approach enables the employee to actively participate in the discussion as well as discover. Questions and silence form the cornerstone of a more nondirective communication and coaching style. Questions reveal what the employee does and doesn't know. The silence, although awkward, punctuates your meaning and resolve in making a point.

The direct vs. indirect coaching styles are contrasted below. One style is not necessarily better than the other. We are simply suggesting that if you lean on one style too much, it gets repetitive and boring for the employee; that goes for the questioning technique too. The employee will at times want you to make direct statements. The comparison and guidelines in Table 6.1 will be helpful.

Table 6.1

Indirect Style	Direct Style
• Use wide-focus questions that avoid "yes" or "no" answers.	• Make clear and simple statements.
• Listen to the employee's responses, but move the discussion to specifics (narrow or funnel the discussion).	• Get to the point quickly.
• Probe for suggestions and build on the employee's ideas.	• Don't soften the impact of the situation with excessive thoughts, explanations, or justifications.
• Restate key points.	• Own your statement – Use "I" instead of "we" and "they".
• Bridge gaps and encourage more conversation("I see," "Uh-huh," "Yes," "Tell me more about that," etc.).	• Use questions that narrow the focus of the discussion.
• Summarize and check for accuracy of understanding.	• Be sensitive to and aware of resistance and withdrawal.
	• Confront resistance – put it into words.
	• Plan to get more information if that's a concern.

Here is a list of specific penetrating questions that can be used with the Eight-Step Coaching Model. These questions will help you gain critical information with a less direct style.

Step 1: "Are you getting enough support from me?"
"What can I do to help you be as successful as possible?"

Step 2: "What do you want to achieve with this project?"
"Where do you think we stand on this assignment?"

Step 3: "How will your current approach help you achieve your goals?"
"What are some of the risks with your current approach?"

Step 4: "What do you think we should try?"
"What will we do if that doesn't work?"

Step 5: "Are you really committed to this new plan?"
"When can you get started?"

Step 6: "Is it something you really want to try?"
"Is there anything you can anticipate that might get in our way or interfere down the road?"

Step 7: "From your point of view, what is riding on this plan?"
"Do you see how important this plan is?"

"A prudent question is one-half of wisdom."
–Francis Bacon
(1561-1626)

Step 8: "When can we meet next?"
"What do you want to start on first?"

SURFACING UNDERLYING ISSUES

In our society, we have grown accustomed to putting transactions in writing to signal our commitment and resolve. Even the computer age may contribute to an era marked by fewer face-to-face or one-on-one verbal interactions. Over time, this trend may affect our oral communication skills and leaders' ability to supportively confront important communication tasks like delegating, coaching, and training employees. This potential problem could affect employees as well as leaders, thereby restricting and interfering with leader/employee interactions.

Put it into words

The art of putting what you think, feel, or see into words is a deceptively simple skill. In fact, after working with thousands of managers in hundreds of companies, we have noticed that the most challenging skill is acting in an authentic and assertive way by effectively converting intentions, thoughts, and feelings into words. Countless times at the conclusion of a role play or a practice coaching session, we have asked why leaders didn't comment or draw attention to some painfully obvious and unavoidable resistance, difference, or misunderstanding. They answered by saying, "I saw it happening. It was crystal clear that the employee didn't believe me, but I didn't know what I should say or do about it," or "I am sure the employee thought I was being difficult or hardheaded about this issue, but I didn't know how to handle the employee's silence."

The most effective way of handling these situations is to clarify and state your intentions, specify the support you want to give, and articulate your expectations. Likewise, when you perceive resistance, reluctance, or misunderstandings, be prepared to go the extra mile and put your observations of the employee's behavior into words. Employees may have a hard time owning up to the fact that they disagree with the leader, and so their feelings show up later in the form of some underlying low-level resistance. In other situations, employees won't confess that the leader's feedback was painful or even devastating to them personally, and so we see the signs and aftermath in the form of defensiveness and argumentation or in passive resistance, such as silence or giving in. If you feel the employee is giving in too easily, stimulate some conversation about it by saying, "You seem to be quite accepting of this," or "I expected you to debate this a little," or "So far, you have agreed with everything I have suggested; somehow I am detecting that you are unsure about this." The key here lies in simply describing the physical signs, rather than interpreting and jumping to conclusions about what they mean. If you are patient, employees will take responsibility and clarify their reactions, emotions, and thoughts.

Describe the physical signs

This procedure not only clarifies your position but can also be used to "smoke out" the employee's honest reactions, thoughts, and feelings. The conversation becomes more genuine and authentic if you take the lead and signal to the employee that his/her honest responses are vital to an effective conversation. This procedure basically communicates to the other person that you value open, honest, and direct discussion. Once the leader has used words to draw some attention to the subtle indicators of the employee's reaction, then the next step is to be silent. This silence serves as a graphic shift of conversation and responsibility; it suggests that the employee express or amplify on your observations. This may make the employee uncomfortable, but if you get no response, repeat the process again. The tension you are creating, if not overdone, will create the urge in the employee to open up more to you. Silence, probably the most under-utilized communication tool in this process, is critical. If the employee begins to disclose or "level" with you, even if only a little, be prepared to offer support for taking a risk and for telling you what he/she is really thinking and feeling. Remember, the clarity and authenticity that you are striving for are a valued element of the coaching discussion.

Be silent

"To say the right thing at the right time, keep still most of the time."
–John W. Roper

The Coach's Contribution
(Positive Game Plan)

THE "ONE MINUTE" LEADER – ONE BIG MYTH

"Employees will judge your supportiveness by your actions as well as your words."

30-45 minutes are needed

From our data and observations, the pattern is strong and clear: highly effective leaders and successful coaching discussions consumed 40% more time than was spent by other leaders in unsuccessful coaching discussions. The evidence shows that 30 to 45 minutes is an appropriate time frame for a fully developed coaching interaction.

There is no question that leaders today are obsessed with saving time because they are under serious time pressures. Organizations require leaders to attend to a lot of routine administrative and sometimes bureaucratic activities such as budget reports, meetings, committees, and community relations. In addition, they have a huge list of reading materials, in-baskets, and professional association responsibilities. The list is endless, and there simply is never enough time to do all that can or should be done. For this reason, it is easy for the leader to lose focus of what a leader really is: a manager of people and their performance, not a manager of paper, projects, equipment, or money. Please don't misunderstand: the management of things is critically important to success in any organization. However, a common mistake that we have observed is that many managers end up taking time from their leadership responsibilities (coaching, directing, delegating, etc.) in order to meet other administrative responsibilities. Some managers have not received the appropriate training or don't have a vision of what leadership really is. They end up filling their days with other activities thereby unintentionally minimizing or neglecting their leadership role and ending up like other managers in the "activity trap."

To address this problem, the writers are proposing some tempting but dangerous options For example, the one-minute approach is being aggressively peddled to managers as a solution to time pressures. The basic idea is that you can reward, reprimand, or engage in other leadership functions literally in one minute. This idea is obviously popular and appealing from a time management point of view. Frankly, we believe that it is preposterous to think of even trying to do coaching in one minute. The reality is that, in terms of a meaningful and effective coaching session, the one-minute notion is pure myth. In coaching employees about existing or potential performance concerns, career opportunities, or positive performance, the leader cannot excessively rush the discussion if real employee support or buy-in is desired. Obviously a number of factors cause the 30 to 45-minute guideline to increase or decrease. For instance, emergency situations, high levels of leader-employee agreement, clarity or simplicity of the solution, high level of employee experience, etc., enable the leader to use less time. On the other hand, differences or conflict, low employee experience, ambiguity, personal sensitivity, complexity, etc., demand a more thorough and expanded discussion. We also know that in some organizations, leaders have to supervise large numbers of employees (more than 8). We encourage you to read the chapter on how time can be saved, without sacrificing quality, in a coaching session.

When a leader says, "I am prepared to take the time necessary for a high-quality discussion," the leader is indirectly supporting and saying to the employee, "I care about you, I care about this issue, I want to see you be successful, I care about your input and perceptions, and I want this concern resolved in more than a superficial way." Patience and courtesy in a coaching discussion are the basic fabric of supportiveness. Speeding up a discussion denotes a need to push or force the issue and may result in increased employee resistance. The bottom line is that a good coaching session is like a quality cheese; it takes more than a minute to develop into a quality product.

DOING YOUR HOMEWORK

A critical difference distinguishes planning from worrying and agonizing about a pending coaching session.

One of the most striking findings from our interviews with leaders and employees was the amount of emphasis given to planning and preparation prior to the coaching discussion. Effective leaders don't make elaborate plans, nor do they spend lengthy periods of time planning. However, they do collect accurate data, anticipate problems, and mentally rehearse key parts. Carried to an extreme, the planning stage can become a source of procrastination or an excuse for putting off the one-to-one problem solving. The primary benefit of planning is its tendency to deflate the emotionally charged nature of some issues. Employees really pick up on the leader's level of preparation, the accuracy of data, and the extent to which the leader is emotional, overly aggressive, or impatient.

Primary benefit

So what does a leader do in order to really prepare for the discussion? Well, here is a plan that we have developed from working with highly successful leaders.

"How to's"

THE GROUNDWORK

In your own mind, define and articulate your expectations and the mission of the employee as soon as possible. You might pretend that you are trying to explain these to a new employee as a way of checking for clarity.

Develop an accurate description of the situation you wish to discuss. Base the description on facts that can be supported.

Write down a few of the key words you plan to use. Ask yourself if they are clear, supportive, and focused on problem solving. Some words may seem very volatile and highly charged to the employee. Try to avoid these.

Because good questions can be more effective than statements, write down two or three central questions to help the employee think about the situation and to stimulate involvement in the discussion. Try to anticipate any blind spots, problems or developmental needs that the employee may be unaware of, and consider how you can illustrate your perceptions and increase awareness.

THE DELIVERY

Be prepared to level with the employee. It isn't uncommon for leaders to be afraid of hurting the feelings of an employee who is typically a good performer. The dilemma is that you will hurt the employee's feelings more and lose his/her respect for you as a leader if you don't shoot straight.

Acknowledge your contribution to the situation. We haven't seen a case yet where the leader didn't play some role. No doubt the outcome was unintended and not totally your fault either, but you can win a lot of points in the employee's mind if you accept your fair share of responsibility.

Describe what types of actions and commitments from the employee would represent a fair beginning with respect to resolving this concern. Don't go overboard and define the entire solution. . .give the employee a little space and a chance to collaborate and develop some ownership in terms of the solution. Remember, we found wide agreement that collaboration is the highest form of support and respect you can show to the employee. What other types of supportive statements can you make that the employee will value and respond to?

REACTIONS

Anticipate and program yourself to react as objectively as possible if your views are challenged. Remember that because you are, in effect, examining and questioning the employee's behavior, the employee may become defensive and feel exposed, which is normal and natural. Don't take the hostility personally.

Plan to listen to the employee's reactions. What does he/she want you to hear? Usually employees feel trapped and victimized by circumstances. It is okay to show some empathy without calling off the problem-solving process.

For additional help in planning for the discussion, see: Thinking It Through — Planning Guide (in the appendix)

"Nothing is more terrible than activity without insight."
– Thomas Carlyle (1795-1881)

ATTENDING TO THE EARLY WARNING SIGNALS

You don't have to be a psychic, just very observant, in order to head off a disaster.

When leaders explain their problems in managing employee performance, we invariably detect that the leaders saw clear indications of the problems emerging well before the situations ever became critical or unavoidable.

Employees are also frequently aware of the signs that indicate trouble ahead. Perhaps the signals were not strong enough to be conclusive, or perhaps the leader was unable to muster up sufficient courage to confront a relatively minor situation.

Watch the blips   In focusing on the topic of early warning signals, we simply suggest that a leader understand radar and not ignore "blips" on the screen. Light, or non-directive, coaching designed mainly to gather information, check the employee's direction and progress, clarify a task, or remind an employee of something to be considered is not scary or dangerous work. In fact, this style of coaching fits in nicely with a regular pattern of healthy and nonthreatening (planned) contacts and meetings with the employee. This way everyone knows that the scanning or radar detection is just as predictable as in an airport control tower.

We have assembled a list of generic early warning signals that have emerged from our consultations with leaders. If any of these conditions are occurring in your day-to-day operations, the signals will emanate externally from the employee, or you will feel them internally (psychological or physiological) in your head, stomach, tight fists, or various other extremities. These signals indicate a need for exploratory coaching which is less tense, less risky, and more proactive in nature.

MANAGEMENT'S EARLY WARNING SIGNALS OF POTENTIAL PROBLEMS/OPPORTUNITIES

A check list   Look over this check list carefully, and see if any of these conditions occur in your day-to-day supervision of this employee.

Employee Signals

- *falls behind and delays progress on assignments*
- *has very vague action plans and strategies for the future*
- *has no specific target completion dates for key assignments*
- *has grossly optimistic estimates and expectations for assignments*
- *submits reports that are increasingly late*

- *shows no initiative to communicate and account for personal results*
- *conducts infrequent visits and updates with you*
- *overlooks or forgets important matters*
- *forgets to return phone calls*
- *becomes defensive in response to your questions and inquiries*
- *tries overselling you on substitutes or shortcuts*
- *lacks attention to or concentration on detail*
- *shows a change in enthusiasm level on assignments*
- *shows an increase in absenteeism or preoccupation with personal matters*
- *makes promises and exaggerations that are unreal*
- *rarely expresses voluntary commitment*
- *rushes too fast to get things done at the last minute*
- *focuses on excuses and justifications for mistakes*
- *makes requests for unusual extensions in deadlines*
- *continually misunderstands your instructions*
- *relies too much on you for ideas and direction*
- *creates infighting or conflicts with other group members*

Manager Signals

- *feel disappointment*
- *discover unexpected surprises*
- *have feelings of uncertainty*
- *experience tension and worrying*
- *constantly second-guess the employee*
- *over-rationalize, hoping and wishing for "luck"*
- *feel confusion*
- *give in too much*

"Ignorance is no excuse – it's the real thing."
– Irene Peter

SEVEN PIECES OF THE PERFORMANCE PUZZLE

Once a leader observes a problem or senses that an issue needs to be discussed with an employee, the leader should consider its possible causes. It is common (well documented

Don't just attribute it to the employee

in other studies) for leaders to excessively attribute the cause to the employee (especially when the issue bears directly on the leader's own performance). We hear leaders say the employee just isn't motivated, committed, or talented enough. While these factors do frequently contribute to problems, we have found that the astute leader examines other contributing factors or characteristics before coming down hard and singling out the employee as the culprit. We have identified and defined seven common characteristics of the situation that could contribute to creating the circumstances faced by the leader and employee in the coaching session.

Other possibilities

1. *Employee motivation, willingness, or desire:* When this appears to be a contributing factor, the leader needs to work at raising the employee's felt need for change or at disturbing the employee's complacency (Step 3). In addition, the leader can point out or draw attention to consequences of fulfilling a plan of action (Step 7). As far as Step 4 is concerned, the leader should make sure the employee's role in the solution is challenging, interesting, and inherently rewarding.

2. *Employee knowledge, skill, or ability:* If this is playing a role in creating or sustaining the situation, the leader needs to consider formal training, guided practice, or feedback on results of the employee's efforts. Remedies can be built into the plan of action (Step 4).

3. *Employee personality match with the job and organization:* If a mismatch exists and employees are too dependent on leaders or tend to be nonconformist to the point of disruption, then the leader needs either to encourage the employee towards more risk taking as part of the action plan or to seek alternative job settings or job structures to insure a more compatible and satisfying situation (all of this is part of Step 4).

4. *Employee blind spots or lack of awareness:* Sometimes the employee is inattentive to performance signals and yardsticks, or they are not available to guide the employee's performance. This simply requires more feedback on progress (Step 2) and putting signals and indicators in place to help employees help themselves in the future (Step 4).

5. *System obstacles, or organizational policies and procedures:* Sometimes the employee encounters cumbersome

policies or procedures that interfere with performance. Other departments or individuals can also create logjams in moving an assignment along. The solution lies in creative alternatives, calculated risks, and back-up plans (Step 4).

6. *Resources:* When time, dollars, equipment, and people are tight, employees experience frustration and lower productivity. Either expectations and standards need to be adjusted (Step 2), or plans for more efficient utilization of resources will have to be developed (Step 4).

7. *Communication breakdown:* Confusion and misunderstanding about priorities, roles, responsibilities, or estimates can create interference and greatly impact employee production.

Leaders need to be sensitive to these seven general areas and prepared to direct the discussion and the coaching steps in a way that will address the key contributing causes. This will help balance responsibility for the problem and prevent exceeding the employee's willingness or ability to perform. Our data suggest that the bigger the problem, the more likely a leader is to focus on the employee's motivation and skill. This creates defensiveness and resistance, and ultimately a severe stress on the relationship and on trust. This backfire effect can be avoided by fairly allocating responsibility for the problem. This doesn't mean letting the employee off the hook. It simply means directing the coaching discussion (information gathering, plans, commitments, etc.) to those contributing factors that will most help to solve the problem.

FOCUSING ON FORM VS. SUBSTANCE

During the data-collection phase of our study, an interesting pattern emerged. The leaders we talked to usually selected a coaching experience in which the employee's form – communication skills, relationships, or individual style – was the central concern. When we talked to employees, they shied away from exposing personal issues and focused instead on substance – task-related problems and performance of the job itself (in other words, quality, errors, or technical difficulties in what they did rather than process issues or problems in how they did their jobs).

This finding lends some credence to the argument that nontechnical or personal issues are more sensitive and per-

"Working with people is difficult, but not impossible."

– Peter Drucker

Personal issues are more sensitive

haps more difficult to discuss because of the personal exposure for the employee. Furthermore, leaders seem to be saying that these issues are extremely relevant and important. It may be that employees underrate the significance of these aspects of their performance. They assume that if the job itself is done well, that's all the manager should care about. Therefore, leaders should be prepared to be as descriptive and precise as possible when bringing up these more subjective topics that are hard to measure. Perhaps leaders need to openly admit to employees that these are difficult, ambiguous, and yet vitally important topics. It will be helpful to the leader to think about examples, to be able to point to others who seem to have mastered the subtleties of the job. Leaders are likely to encounter employee resistance to changing per-

Expect resistance

sonal habits and styles that may have been acceptable in the past or at least not objectionable. These days growth, especially upward or lateral career mobility, depends less on proving technical competencies and more on demonstrating leadership skills (social, positive, political). Employees need coaching and clarification from leaders that total effectiveness entails more than mere efficiency in performing the basic job. This is a dramatic revelation to many employees. Improvement may require gentle persistence on the leader's, and certainly results will be slower to develop and less detectable than in the more quantifiable area of job productivity.

THE OVERLOAD PROBLEM

Once leaders have built up the courage to confront employees in a constructive dialogue, their tendency is to overload or dump too many issues on the employee. Because many issues may have built up, once leaders have the employee in a coaching session, they like to clear the deck of all of the issues. This creates pressure that has to be managed in a patient or disciplined way. If the leader opens the floodgates of unresolved issues, he/she runs the risk of sounding punitive and resentful rather than solution oriented. Nearly

Focus on one or two issues

75% of the employees that we have talked to during our research indicated that they would prefer leaders who focus on one or two issues, at most, in a coaching discussion. Keep in mind that individual differences do enter the picture because a few hardy souls (approximately 10% of the employees) preferred that leaders hold no issues in reserve.

When the leader meets the employee face to face, it seems, on the surface, that the natural and mature thing to do is just lay all the cards on the table. However, if the leader is really focused on the coaching process, then the availability of time and energy dictates that only one issue, or two at most, be discussed and resolved as fully as possible. Simply put, most employees have a finite capacity or threshold that enables them to focus, absorb, and remember limited amounts of information and plans generated during the coaching session. By dumping on employees, you rob them of the hope and motivation that you want to create in order to change things in the future. This is one reason why employees get frustrated in the annual performance appraisal when so many topics and so much performance have to be discussed.

Stay focused

Remember, the goal of a coaching session is to make the employee comfortable in working through one issue with you in a routine and relatively informal process. Furthermore, you stand a better chance of creating a positive snowball effect if you can establish a pattern of success with one issue. Be cautious if the employee urges you to unload. He/she may be trying to prove to you the capability of handling a lot of feedback rather than of doing something about the issues. If the employee wants to turn the coaching session into a dumping session, take a firm stand about putting a cap on the issue. Indicate that from time to time you would like to discuss other relevant issues, but for this time period, you believe it is important to focus on the one concern that has been raised. Tell the employee that you recognize that other issues are important; then ask when a good time would be to talk some more. Thank the employee for his/her assistance and contribution regarding the initial concern and wish him/her sincere good luck on carrying out the action plans.

WINNING MENTAL ATTITUDE

The Dilemma of the Inherited Employee

Imagine that your boss just handed you a fat promotion. That's the good news. The bad news is that your new assignment is to head up a unit that has been struggling for two years. Your boss graciously relieved the previous manager of his assignments with these unsettling words, "I don't know how we are going to get along without you, but starting Monday we are going to try!" Realizing that you are going into a difficult situation we made sure that the Good Witch of the North happened along and granted you three wishes for your unit. What will yours be?

Three wishes

We will refund the purchase price of this book if you didn't include the freedom to build your own staff of employees. But, in reality, you will end up working with some employees who are already in place. Will your approach be different for these two groups of employees? Most of us would like to believe we would treat everyone equally and consistently. However, the information we have gathered suggests that managers treat inherited employees differently than voluntarily selected employees. We call this phenomenon the *inheritance effect*. Managers tend to affiliate with employees they select or hire and disaffiliate with those employees they inherit as part of an existing organization.

The inheritance effect

The relationship is more often perceived by both managers and employees as positive and supportive when employees are hired by the manager. For inherited employees, establishing a supportive relationship can be more difficult, and a critical, pessimistic climate may prevail. In fact, the leader may attribute problems in the organization to the existing work force and be instantly critical of employee performance. The inheritance effect represents the difference between the known and the unknown. The leader knows the limits and capabilities and the extent to which the known employee can be trusted; the leader counts on this employee's support. For those employees who were already on board in the organization, the leader may be a little suspicious until the employees prove themselves over and over again.

Support is harder when you didn't hire them

With regard to coaching situations, this mindset results in a self-filling prophecy: When asked to describe negative coaching situations, 70% of the responses we received concerned employees whom the manager inherited. Two-thirds of the positive coaching situations were with employees the manager had hired. We believe this is due to a feeling of loyalty, a need to develop those hired, and a desire to validate the correctness of the original selection decision. For inherited employees, the manager is more critical; and with a lack

Self-fulfilling prophecy

of a positive, supportive relationship, the counseling sessions can more easily turn out to be negative or punitive, or the manager can come on too strong.

The following suggestions may help overcome the inheritance effect:

How to
overcome this

1. List the positive and negative behaviors you associate with each employee working for you. For those employees whom you inherited, do the negatives outweigh the positives, or are there some serious concerns on the list? If so, and you don't feel good about this conclusion, continue.

2. For each inherited employee, analyze whether the listed negative behaviors are based on your own actual observations, assumptions from the past, or hearsay evidence.

3. For those negative behaviors based on assumptions, define a way of assessing whether these are truly negative behaviors or just a function of your disaffiliative mindset. Some examples include work projects, discussions with the employee, or an honest reassessment on your part.

4. To reverse the self-filling prophecy, establish a course of action to build a positive relationship with your inherited employees:

> Get to know these people better.
>
> Make sure they know that you are a supportive leader (clarify this with them). Don't tackle too many issues or concerns at once.
>
> Be absolutely sure that you have supporting data if you do have a concern.
>
> Give them recognition and acknowledge their contributions.
>
> Try to conduct positive and motivational coaching sessions. (See Chapter 9.)

Exercise
patience

The main thing we are suggesting is that the leader needs to exercise extra precaution when coaching the inherited employee. To put it simply, the leader may not perceive these employees as positively as those selected, and the employee may detect a hint of hostility unless the leader pays extra attention to supportive behaviors.

COURAGE AND THE AGONY OF COACHING

Coaching an employee on a sensitive and personal topic

"We must have courage to bet on our ideas, to take the calculated risk, and to act. Everyday living requires courage if life is to be effective and bring happiness."
– Alaxwell Mattz

like performance or contribution to the organization can be as difficult and agonizing as telling a young son or daughter about sex. You end up playing the same mental games in your head over and over again: "What should they be told? How much do they already know? (Or how much do they want me to think they know?) How much detail do I go into?" When you are unable to answer these penetrating questions, you put the task off for another six months. Eventually, you discover the harsh reality that there is very little they are unaware of, but a lot they don't know.

Everyone feels uncomfortable

Nearly everyone feels uncomfortable when coaching employees, yet few are willing to admit that they feel ambivalent or inadequate. Many leaders who say, with some pride, that they have no hesitation tend to approach the job like a bulldozer (overly aggressively). In fact, coaching is risky (you may lose control of the situation), and you are vulnerable (you have to substantiate your case, and your leadership style may be questioned by the employee). Consequently you exaggerate your worst fears, you get uptight, you worry the night before the discussion is to take place, and you try to figure out ways to avoid or postpone it. But deep down, you know this isn't a helpful strategy.

Most people favor directness, candor (trust), and honesty, as well as efficiency, excellence, and quality. But these goals cannot be met unless leaders are more willing to set aside ambivalence and hesitation, and to trust that the skills and ideas presented in this book will work.

Rationalization

Many leaders rationalize that the issue or concern isn't worth the time or effort of a coaching session. But this comes back to haunt them later when the employee's work is put under the microscope of others (their boss, customers, regulatory agencies, etc.). This occurs when a new position is to be filled that is an advancement for the employee, at performance appraisal time, and during the crucial high-exposure stages of an important project. At these times, earlier hesitation ends up costing both the leader and the employee very directly.

Why leaders resist the discussion

We have heard many explanations and rationalizations about why leaders resist speaking with employees more frequently about progress and problems. The reality is that no one wants to hurt people or jeopardize their performance in areas that are meeting or exceeding expectations. Leaders go about insulating themselves from facing the reality that a meaningful discussion will help improve things. So leaders do the following:

- *hope for a miracle, that things will get better without any intervention.*
- *pray that the employee will gain some enlightened self-awareness.*
- *worry that any action or discussion will only make matters worse.*
- *rationalize or discount the concern by taking other things (areas of successful performance) into account.*
- *believe that they can hobble along and get by with minimal damage.*
- *fret that the issue will get escalated or that the employee will resent them and attack back.*
- *realize, painfully, that they have made mistakes too and have little right to be pointing the finger at others. This puts leaders in an awkward position when they advocate changes and improvements in others (the ill-equipped-judge syndrome).*
- *feel doubts about their own ability to orchestrate and guide a really productive discussion (especially if emotions enter the picture).*

Leaders need to just accept that, to some extent, resisting potentially difficult situations is normal and natural. Then they need to make sure that these perceptual obstacles do not get in the way. Simply anticipate your own hesitations and ambivalence. Tell yourself over and over again that it is okay, and simply move forward and trust the eight-step coaching process to work if you carefully attend to each step.

"To do nothing is in every man's power."
– Samuel Johnson (1709-1784)

THE UNDERLYING COACHING EXPERIENCE

Before a leader engages an employee in a coaching experience, he/she should decide what experience or mindset is to be created for the employee.

The leader can effectively utilize the coaching session to establish a critical foundation for the employee's experience with coaching – by this we mean the way the employee perceives the coaching experience in terms of key thoughts,

What do you want to create?

emotions, and intentions. Regardless of the topic, agreements, commitments, timetables, etc., the employee will leave the coaching session with new data, opinions, and a frame of mind about the leader. Because leaders benefit from some planning and forethought prior to meeting with the employee, we need to consider the range of responses that may impact the coaching session. An employee may be left, at any point, between the following extremes, depending on the experience that you create:

content/comfortable	*challenged/pressured*
informed/awakened	*confused/in the dark*
free	*closed in*
confident	*embarrassed*
supported	*abandoned*
empowered	*scared/frightened*
excited/enthused	*depressed*
aware	*unaware*
okay	*chewed out*
feeling accepted	*feeling rejected*
protected	*exposed*
rewarded/encouraged	*punished*
involved in a collaboration	*manipulated*
personally close	*personally distant*
considered	*offended*

The climate of the underlying experience should help guide the discussion style and the way a leader develops a plan of action, offers feedback, seeks commitment, and manages resistance. The process of creating a primary experience requires that the leader put into words his/her intentions and then follow through in a consistent manner as each step is presented. Employees usually remember the quality and nature of their primary experience for longer than the specific topic, actions, or timetables designed to address the particular issue or concern. The employee reaction and interpretation of the experience influence how cooperative and enthusiastic the employee will be in future coaching sessions.

The key is to practice putting the intended primary experience into words. For example, if the leader wants the employee enthused about resolving the concern or issue, the leader simply needs to make three good-faith efforts to say it.

1. "I hope you will really get behind and support the action plan."

2. "Your enthusiasm, on this issue, will make all the difference in the world."

3. "I hope you leave here feeling as enthusiastic and optimistic as I am."

The bottom line is that if employees understand what the lasting impression is that the leader is trying to create, they will feel less manipulated and more supported. Furthermore, the underlying experience may leave an impression on the employee that will last a long time. The leaders can achieve better results from a coaching session if they will make a conscious choice about how they want to frame and position the main theme of the coaching experience.

PROACTIVE VS. REACTIVE COACHING

When leaders describe their concerns to us, we can usually divide them into two groups: either the leaders are looking ahead (proactive) and seeking out cues that performance is not meeting expectations, or they are looking backward (reactive) to a difficult situation that has already happened. Both situations require coaching, either to prevent the further development of problems or to correct and salvage what remains from a more critical emergency and to prevent future occurrences.

Don't analyze the wake of the ship.

We contend that it is easier and more effective to engage in preliminary problem solving or exploratory Type-I coaching than it is to do hard-core problem solving after behavior is imbedded in time and habit – not to mention the higher emotions involved. Type-I coaching is good during the early stages of a concern because it focuses on more nondirective information gathering, reaffirmation of plans and commitments, and discussion of potential obstacles. Type-I coaching has certain advantages in terms of saving money and time, and employee learning. When concerns are handled before they blossom into full-fledged problems, stress is also reduced on the leader and employee.

Type-I Coaching

Type-II Coaching

When Type-I coaching doesn't work or when this strategy has been overlooked, then a more intense problem-solving approach should be used. This usually requires a more direct application of all of the coaching skills, including a more direct style of communication. There is nothing wrong with Type-II coaching: in fact, it is what we usually think of when times are difficult. Type-II coaching simply requires more rigor in completion of all the steps during the coaching process. If leaders are alert to signs indicating an emerging issue and do not procrastinate, rationalize that the issue is too minor, or excuse the employee because of other positive and offsetting attributes and behaviors, Type-I coaching may diminish the need for Type-II coaching. A commitment to proactive coaching will help ease the coaching burden and reduce the need for crisis management.

COACHING: A PROCESS NOT AN EVENT

"Who left this silver bullet?"

By now, the reader will have sensed that coaching is more than sitting down one to one with an employee and discussing issues or concerns. Important preliminary events, like planning and data gathering, are followed by the main event or coaching discussion itself, and then by subsequent events like follow-up and support. It is important to view coaching as a process and not a single event, because people don't change suddenly. Change and improvement in job performance evolve; people like to explore, test out, and pilot new behaviors, plans, or actions. Employees may even want to resist or test your resolve, commitment, or seriousness before they become serious and committed.

Evolution, not revolution

There is no question that leaders who are willing to engage in coaching on a regular basis are likely to achieve greater results over time than leaders who do not. A coaching discussion itself provides a focus and a source of accountability that do not occur in the other coaching phases. Unfortunately, too many books and training programs seduce you into believing that coaching is as simple as three easy steps, or that it can be done in one minute, or that you can do it by watching 25 short TV episodes of Hollywood actors and then mimicking their actions. These advocates treat coaching as an event, and they don't focus on the dynamics of the coaching process. We feel that by viewing coaching as a process and change as an evolutionary process, leaders will avoid false expectations and impatience won't build. All too often we have seen leaders show anger and resentment toward the employee when change doesn't occur as quickly or completely as the leader would like.

Frustration, anger, and resentment are probably the top three enemies of successful coaching. Unlike a specific event, the beginning and end of a process are ill defined. A leader may become annoyed at the ambiguous structure when he/she considers a process view of coaching. A more detailed comparison may be helpful:

Don't get frustrated-- change takes time.

	EVENT OR PROCESS			
	Complexity	**Structure/form**	**Complexity**	**Change**
Process	*Issues and concerns are more complex*	*Steps of the process are cyclical and interactive*	*Long-run payoff and impact*	*Steady, deep, and lasting change*
Event	*Issues and concerns are less complex*	*Steps are linear and sequential*	*Short-run immediate payoff and impact*	*Sudden, immediate surface change*

Leaders need to think in terms of a series of coaching interventions and plan the content and intensity accordingly. It simply isn't realistic to make coaching a one-shot effort and then relax.

Not a one shot effort

8

Coaching Lessons from the World Of Sports

Most of us either participate in, attend, praise, or criticize sporting events. When we watch the local news we learn about at least three things: current events, weather, and sports. There are several 24-hour sports television channels, and an endless number of 24-hour call in radio sports talk shows and web sites. The Super Bowl, the Final Four, the Olympics, Wimbledon, the U.S. Open, the New York Ballet, Monday Night Football, Little League, synchronized swimming, and youth soccer are but a few examples of how sports affect all of our lives. Most people can recall one person – a coach in sports, school, theater, or civic activities – who had a significant impact on their lives. Sports are ever present, and the coaches of these athletes and teams may provide lessons for becoming even better coaches.

Coaches make impact on lives

In athletics, what is your image of the successful coach? Do you picture the bullying, screaming sideline coach or the supportive, helping observer of an Olympic gymnast? Unfortunately, the former is the coach who is most often highlighted by the press. Without identifying specific coaches, the following descriptions and comments about coaches have been gleaned from various Sports Illustrated articles.

"Coaches want to be in control. . . .people like police officers, military people, and people in sports—careers where competitiveness and aggressiveness and control are dominant—tend to get involved in spousal abuse."

"_____ is inflexible, stubborn, and aloof, rarely praises and frequently criticizes his players and doesn't even remember their names. . . .a Jekyll and Hyde personality. If I get in the Hall of Fame you can bet I won't have him presenting me the trophy."

"This is a game for madmen said _____, maybe the greatest coach and madman of all. The perfect name for the perfect coach would be Simple Simon Legree."

"_____ refused to talk about _____. 'A subject I would rather not discuss'. But is it known that _____had difficulty abiding the coach's abusive and insulting treatment of him."

Is the person changing? In business, the role of coach is being redefined. Contrast these comments and descriptions with the following:

"The coach must account for his ego, that is being distracted by your own importance. Successful coaches realize that winning teams are not run by single individuals who dominate the scene and reduce the rest of the group to marionettes. Winning teams are more like open forums in which everyone participates in the decision making process, coaches and players alike, until the decision is made"[1].

During his first practice, John Wooden, retired head basketball coach for UCLA, handed out and discussed his 13-point pyramid of success. During his tenure the UCLA basketball team accomplished the best winning record in sports. Do these 13 points deal with the techniques of basketball? Surprisingly, not one focuses on "X's" and "O's." They capture what Mr. Wooden had developed as key personal and life values and include loyalty, self-control, poise, alertness, sacrifice, hard work, and initiative In later years, many of his star athletes recall this foundation as one that helped them beyond the basketball court. His players also marveled that he never talked about winning – just doing your best. In pre-game warm-ups, Wooden sat relaxing on the bench, not "motivating", because he wanted his team relaxed when the initial whistle blew. His were hardly the screaming sideline antics we have come to associate with coaches.

As this quote and story suggest, the coach-athlete, like the manager-employee, relationship is changing from the master-apprentice model to an ongoing committed partnership model. Whether professional or sandlot, the athlete of today demands not the tyrannical coach of days past but the supportive, helping partner. This transition has not been com-

Successful coaches

Ongoing committed partnership

pleted in the sporting arena. Both business and sports organizations still have coaches/managers who operate from an
autocratic style. We believe, however, that this kind of coach
is in a shrinking minority. Business leaders can learn much
from the new, successful, and effective sports coach of today.
Yet, modeling all our behaviors after those of sports coaches
is impossible and impractical. Take those things that sports
coaches do that improve their effectiveness and try applying
them to the business environment. Where this is impossible,
e.g. spending 100% of your time coaching, develop a more
realistic strategy. Successful sports coaches' passion/love of
the game is a powerful attribute for any coach.

The world of amateur athletics recognizes, just like business organizations, the importance of the right coaching
behaviors. The United States Olympic Committee has determined that athletic ability is distributed fairly evenly
thoughtout the world. The determining competitive factor is
not athletic ability but the coaching those athletes receive.
To that end clinics are being developed to teach people the
right coaching behaviors at all levels of sports. Is the coaching your employees receive the determining competitive factor for your business?

HOW IS THE SPORTS COACH DIFFERENT
FROM THE BUSINESS COACH?

Athletes versus employees. Most athletes are young, open to
improvement, eager to learn, and anxious to receive what a
coach can provide. For the athlete, there is a defined season
and something tangible to compete for. Feedback is automatic, immediate, and specific, and athletes can change
coaches and/or teams. Employees, on the other hand, aren't
always as emotionally committed. When have you seen an
adult cry or rant and rage when a goal was not achieved? For
employees, feedback and performance are hard to quantify.
Work goes on; there is no end and only vague score cards.
Lastly, employees do not demand coaching or search critically for improvement. Without belaboring the point or
making value judgments, suffice it to say that the two are
different in their values, motivations, and needs. However,
these differences do not change what constitutes effective
coaching behaviors. The application of the Eight-Step
Coaching Model may differ, but the concepts will not. All

coaches, for example, need to create a supportive, trusting relationship, (Step One). Further, all coaches need to create the internal motivation or felt need to pursue a more effective course of action, (Step Two). Athletes, like employees, are driven by the same basic needs.

Sports coaches versus business coaches. In sports, the coach can rarely outperform those coached, while in business the coach may be an accomplished player. One of the most successful coaches in the National Basketball Association never played professional basketball. Is it possible to conceive of a successful sales manager who never was a salesperson? In sports, coaching is a full-time job supported in many cases with assistant coaches; in business the coach has many diverse responsibilities. In gymnastics the coach's span of control is many times one-on-one. The number of "suits" on the bench, during a college basketball game, often equals or outnumbers the "uniforms" or actual players. Athletes can practice before the game and take time-outs; in business the clock is always running. Most athletic coaches see themselves as, first and foremost, teachers. Even though the word "coach" has become a popular addition to most managers' job descriptions, we doubt that many would also include teacher. So the playing field and conditions are different. We believe that there are some unique lessons to be learned and applied to business.

WHAT BUSINESS COACHES CAN ADOPT FROM SUCCESSFUL SPORT COACHES.

Determine what type of team is needed. Is there a unique product or "value added" by the team that goes beyond a sum of the parts? A colleague has helped more than one team by asking its members to define the unique product of the team – why are they here, what would their direct reports be willing to pay them to produce as a team? What is the leverage that this group can have only by working together as a group? If none, you will coach individuals and coordinate information exchange meetings.

In working with a division manager for a major research and development organization, it became apparent that the unit managers' responsibilities were so diverse that this group collectively was a team in name only. The major function was to exchange information and handle the transfer of knowledge and people across the units to best achieve the overall objectives of the division. Rather than agonize over why this team wasn't functioning, it became more relevant to recognize that they didn't really need to be a team, to define those tasks or areas that required information exchange, and leave it at that. Their team meetings became more productive once this issue was settled.

Define the type of team

If this team could produce a unique product, then defining the type of team and resulting interaction needed would be productive. To borrow an analogy from the world of sports, is a baseball, football, or basketball team appropriate? The baseball team has skillful players at separate positions with no more than three interacting on a given play. The key to success is that communications between players are clear and consistent. The football team also relies on players skillful in only one or two positions; an offensive tackle could not be a defensive back. This team requires integration and coordination of movements; they move as one force down the field, following a set game plan. The basketball team is illustrative of an interdependent team; players are totally interchangeable, constantly dependent on one another. Decisions are made at the moment with very few "plays" sent in from the sideline. The interdependence and integration of effort are as important as individual athletic ability. Which type of team is appropriate will impact how the team players need to interact.

What percent

Make coaching a high priority. Okay, so it's not 100% of your job. What percent is it? A major financial institution has a performance expectation that managers will spend 20% of their time coaching others. The majority of people we talk to feel they don't have an adequate amount of time to devote to coaching others. The sports coach would suggest that you delegate some work so you can coach more and develop assistants and trainers who can relieve you of some of your tasks. How many have thought of themselves as the "head coach"? What areas are you going to specialize in, and in what areas will you develop "assistant coaches" to help others on your team? You can't pretend; if you are a coach you are required to put in the time.

Where should the "head" coach spend his or her time? The sports coach would say recruiting and evaluating talent, developing a game plan, helping motivate players toward achieving the vision, demonstrating the commitment to their players, and dealing with the public is where the time is spent. Would your approach to coaching differ if after every big project or new initiative you had to meet the press? Probably not, if you were confident that you had either the right people in the right job or a training and development plan in place for each to exceed the minimum expectations of the job; and in addition, if you knew that all your employees understood, valued, and were committed to the vision, expectations, and objectives for your team, and if a trusting relationship existed between you and every member of your team. Evaluating how you stack up as the "head coach" would be valuable regardless of your level in the organization.

How do you stack up?

Tommy Lasorda, head coach of the Los Angeles Dodgers for 20 years, said, "My responsibility is to get 25 guys playing for the name on the front of their shirts and not the one on the back."

Model the applicable sports coaching behaviors. Take time-outs to assess individual and team effectiveness. Practice or trial run new approaches and/or new ideas whenever possible. Keep everyone informed, and coach in a way that is respectful; never demean a team player. Create a decision-making process in which people feel they can participate, and don't hand off the tough decisions to assistant coaches.

Build a coaching climate. On every sports team there are informal leaders who coach others on the team. Do the members of your team feel an obligation and responsibility to coach you, their teammates, and peers? The concept of 360° feedback is gaining in popularity. As a system, this formalizes the process of obtaining and utilizing multiple sources of information for evaluation and improvement. Only the coach/manager can instill the philosophy which makes this a valuable exercise. It goes beyond the formal once-a-year assessment to a day-to-day way of life. Do your teammates and you expect and accept feedback, coaching, and help from one another? Or do they expect coaching to be only your role? Watch a basketball game at any level – the coach is mostly encouraging team members to support others. The players on the floor are constantly interacting and changing to meet the demands of the game. They are truly

Build a coaching climate

interdependent, coaching and communicating at all times. They don't look to the head coach for all the decisions.

In our sports-dominated society, the athletic metaphor has value for business coaches. There are many great athletic coaches, some never gaining the public attention and national monument status. Learn from their approach, recognizing that their situation and players are unique. Those who are living a committed partnership model have the most to teach.

---

[1]"To Build a Winning Team: An Interview with Head Coach Bill Walsh." By Richard Rapaport. *Harvard Business Review,* January -February, 1993.

9

Positive Motivational Coaching

THE CASE FOR POSITIVE MOTIVATIONAL COACHING

One important point needs clarifying: coaching goes beyond problem solving. Many people misinterpret coaching as only a corrective process aimed at specific errors and deficiencies of an individual. Coaching doesn't always have to be driven by problems; challenges, opportunities, and obstacles that transcend any one member of the organization can be the motivating force. This type of coaching is very exciting to do. It is less personalized in nature and therefore not as stressful or tense, although it does require certain skills and characteristics. Many of the same coaching skills, mindset, and approaches used in problem solving can be applied to positive coaching, which is designed to empower employees to go farther and contribute in new ways.

Beyond Problem Solving

Empower employees

We have found it hard to motivate some leaders to take responsibility for positive coaching seriously. Many leaders tell us, "I don't have any problems with my employees. They are all good people, they work hard and pull their own weight, and frankly I can't think of a thing I would change or talk to them about."

If we had a dollar for every time we have heard this comment, we would be basking in the sun in Hawaii rather than writing this book. Managers think they are "off the hook" because they see nothing to change, correct, or improve upon. They couldn't be further from the truth. In reality, these fortunate leaders need to be as active in their coaching role as is the leader who is beset with enormous problems. In fact, wise leaders are extremely active when things are going

No time to rest

well. They coach and confer with employees on how to maintain and sustain the current state of affairs or develop strategies on how to move closer to their visions and values. In short, good leaders are not satisfied with acceptable performance. Leaders cannot be silent. To achieve the full potential and maximize employee contributions, leaders need some restless dissatisfaction with the status quo, to encourage others to reach new heights. Whatever leaders and their units achieve will be the product of the behavior of those who work for them.

The fact of the matter is organization downsizing, fewer promotional opportunities, career plateaus, increasing numbers of professional employees, and good performers with no specific performance problems are all realities of modern organization life that contribute to the need for positive coaching. Since problem-solving coaching sessions produce a certain amount of stress, it is easy to think that most of the manager's time will be spent in this type of session, but this is not necessarily the case at all.

75% of the time will be positive coaching

To put the two types of sessions into proper perspective, we believe effective managers will spend 75% of their coaching time in positive sessions. The reason we emphasize the problem-solving session in our writing and workshops is because this is more challenging, it's confronting, and it will tax the leader's skills and patience heavily.

In Table 9.1, the two types of sessions are compared:

Table 9.1

Positive Coaching	Problem-Solving Coaching
DEFINITION:	
A review of those things the employee is doing well or opportunities for growth and enrichment.	A meeting to plan for improved performance in a specific area.
GOALS:	
Increased motivation, growth in the partnership.	Behavior change, correction, and adjustments.
TIME FOCUS:	
Future.	Here and now.
LEADER'S ROLE:	
To understand how to better fulfill and support employee needs and current efforts. To take wise risks and contribute more.	To guide, facilitate, initiate, and manage the problem-solving process. To improve the current situation and help develop a satisfactory direction.

The two types of sessions are different in intent, but the skills and steps of the coaching model apply to both.

The last message the leader wants to send to his or her employees is that they are being neglected or not appreciated, or that their input is not valued. Leaders must understand, and act on the fact, that employees like to grow, achieve, learn, and develop. Believing that an ideal state of affairs can last forever is sheer folly; all organizations and employees have room to develop and grow.

Don't neglect them

So what do leaders do? Well, they need to engage the employee in a positive motivational coaching session designed to address these issues of maintenance and further growth in open dialogue. Let us be clear. We are not talking about career growth necessarily, but about growth in the existing job, expansion, creativity, empowerment to contribute more, and job enrichment. The main task of leaders is to communicate to their employees that they are interested, that they recognize a fine effort when they see it, and that they want to know how they and their employees can work together to sustain what they have or to empower the employees to go for a bigger piece of the action. This becomes a powerfully motivating act because, once again, the message is, "I want you to be a partner in the organization." It says that, as leaders, you are interested in your employees' futures and in making sure everyone is supported with resources and guidance. It reinforces the importance of the employees' needs, and so everyone should benefit in the long run. This type of coaching is a strong investment in building a relationship that will last far into the future.

What to do

From the information collected and the leaders observed, we have compiled a list of skills and attitudes possessed by strong positive coaches:

Here's what effective coaches do

1. They have a clear vision of what they want from their organization. They can articulate their values about the organization and are not afraid to do so.

2. They feel like they can control their future and demonstrate excitement about tackling problems and challenges (restless energy).

3. They know they can't solve all the challenges alone; they value teamwork.

4. They are willing to take intelligent risks and experiment with new approaches; they value creativity.

5. They don't over-control employees, and they give others permission to try out innovative approaches to create ideas and develop their own abilities.

6. They share information and communicate frequently on a one-to-one basis.

7. They accept responsibility for conditions in the group, and they respect the ideas of others (value collaboration).

8. They can describe and articulate the challenges and goals for the group, outline expectations and roles of members, establish timetables for assignments, follow up and maintain accountability, and encourage and reinforce the contributions of others.

The eight coaching steps that help employees change and improve are very compatible with the attitudes and skills outlined above. Our theory is that if you are an effective problem solver, you can be an effective positive coach. It requires some refocusing, but most importantly it requires a commitment to invest in this type of relationship.

DEVELOPMENTAL COACHING/ACHIEVING YOUR POTENTIAL
The End of the Line

Use the Eight Steps

We often run the risk of implying that the Eight Step Coaching Model is for corrective coaching only, whereas many leaders and organizations are interested in developmental coaching. In fact, the eight-step process is equally effective in developmental situations. Let's first talk about what developmental coaching means.

For us, it represents the last frontier of coaching. It is the point at which employees are more fully functional, where you do the final tuning in terms of helping to create completely trustworthy, totally responsible, entrepreneurial partners in your operation. As we see it, you are now doing a type of coaching that encourages the employees to take more and wiser risks, to engage in more self-expression, and to discover what lasting contribution they can make. This is a confidence-building process and a creative stage for employees – a chance for them to define a personal mission beyond simple organizational advancement. The beauty of developmental coaching is that it doesn't require advancement and promotion. What you are doing is freeing them up so they can

Freeing up the employee

give employees a personal promotion and maximize their self-esteem.

The primary focus of developmental coaching is helping the employee as well as you, the leader, discover and build toward certain goals:

Goals

1. A job that has adequate variety, meaning, and usefulness (through a process of informally enriching the employee's work itself).

2. Establishment of a future-oriented mission or set of values and definition of a lasting commitment for the employee.

3. Increased self-expression, creativity, and responsible risk taking.

4. Sound relationships, integrity, and the sharing of knowledge and skills with others (being honest and authentic).

You can probably tell by now that developmental coaching is aimed at releasing all of the employees' potential. It requires that you do certain things:

What to do

Trust them more.

Give them more responsibility.

Defer to them more frequently (judgment).

Help them define their values and purpose more clearly (includes inviting employees to express their personal wishes in a dramatic and even radical way so their thoughts can simply be heard and defined).

Let them try some new ideas; give them space to contribute within the rules. Surrender a little control and allow them to act like partners in the business.

If others act jealous, coach them, problem solve, and let them know that it isn't an exclusive club or inner circle reserved for a select few.

If this sounds like a set of personal mottoes or a personal policy statement, you are right on track.

The challenge for the leader is that many employees do feel stuck. They don't know what to do if they are not moving rapidly in a vertical direction in the company. Your task is to help them achieve their fullest potential right where they are, to get them to look at growth and development in

Doesn't require a promotion

a different way. Many employees will need help to see this opportunity. Culture has taught them that growth, contribution, and satisfaction come only when you are living on "Mahogany Row" or in the organizational stratosphere.

By now, you may be feeling some sense of inadequacy as to your ability to help employees find themselves and to discover new ways of contributing to their job and the organization. That is only natural, mainly because all of us are in the same boat as the employees in one way or another. We all could use some positive developmental coaching, and we all wish we had a fully adequate leader who could skillfully help us.

So what do you do? What strategy or approach can be taken with employees who are not in need of corrective coaching? The main points have already been covered. You simply need to stick with the steps that have been outlined. Maintain a strong supportive stance as well as initiating action and discussion of the nontraditional opportunities and challenges that lie ahead.

How to use the Eight Steps

The main thing that changes in your coaching strategy is simply the content of each step, rather than its purpose or intent. The following illustrates the modifications in each step:

Step 1

Step 1: Emphasize collaboration in finding a solution for the challenge. Acknowledge the employee's value and contribution to date. Stress your commitment to the employee's growth and satisfaction. Make necessary resources available as much as possible. Listen, be understanding, and offer support throughout the discussion.

Step 2

Step 2: Present the issue as an opportunity rather than an acute problem. Encourage the employee to express what he/she wants, values, and hopes for. Indicate where things could be done differently and new areas where the employee could branch out.

Step 3

Step 3: Go easy on this step. Simply indicate that while the current situation isn't creating any direct pain for you or the organization, it may create some future unrest, boredom, and stagnation for the employee if some changes and initiatives are not started now.

Step 4

Step 4: Open up some discussion on ways of challenging the employee or making life at work more interesting and rewarding. Specifically, explore some informal job design changes that would give the employee more variety, challenge, and responsibility. Try to get the employee involved and participating more. Figure out ways for the employee's knowledge and skills to be shared with others. Help the employee define and articulate a personal mission, policies, and values so he/she can perform and act so as to support them. Determine where the employee might be more creative and innovative, and where some responsible risks could be taken.

Step 5: No change here – ask for a commitment, as always!

Step 6: Be on the lookout for excuses and resistance because change and some unknowns may be uncomfortable to deal with at first.

Step 7: Clarify the future advantages, benefits, and positive consequences of the new direction and action plans.

Step 8: Be prepared to follow up. This change will be just as challenging and difficult as correcting a problem. The employee can easily lose sight of what the two of you are trying to achieve. By hanging in there, you are demonstrating your support and commitment. Plan to check on the progress of this experiment after a very short period of time. Close with a supportive statement.

Step 5

Step 6

Step 7

Step 8

COACHING THE ABOVE-AVERAGE EMPLOYEE OR OUTSTANDING PERFORMER

One of our biggest fears is that a leader will hesitate to coach strong performers who rarely need to be coached. We, in fact, have the same dilemma in our own organization. We probably could get along quite nicely by smoothing over the small or infrequent issues with these employees. The truth is above-average employees do, on occasion, create a problem; and they do want developmental coaching. Consequently, the biggest disservice is done to the employee and not to ourselves. These high-achieving employees are trying to tell us indirectly, by the quality of their work, that they want to be helpful and feel responsible for doing the best possible job.

You need to approach these employees a bit differently

Everyone needs coaching

than other employees. In all likelihood, they are knowledge-able, skillful, and self-motivated; and their own personality style probably fits the organization. We find that when a concern or issue develops, it results from factors other than those listed above, because the employees want to work effectively, are talented, and aren't into nonconformity. The only remaining causes of performance problems are percep-tual blind spots (the employee made an error and didn't real-ize it), confusion and misunderstanding (the employee did-n't understand that the assignment was his/hers), or inade-quate resources (the employee didn't have adequate time, money, equipment, or personnel to do the job). The good news is that these problems are easier to deal with when you have talented, motivated, and compatible employees on your side. The bad news is that you, as the leader, must fulfill your coaching obligation and not allow these employees to blind-ly plod along thinking all is well on the home front.

We suggest that leaders seriously consider a less directive coaching session with highly talented employees. Since you have so many advantages in your favor, you need merely guide the process using questions and nonaggressive state-ments, along with a lot of collaboration and support. We can't say this too strongly: the more hard working and sin-cere the employee, the more you must be prepared to artic-ulate various forms of support during the dialogue so the employee doesn't feel attacked, devalued, and unappreciated. This will prevent the unwanted side effects of a bad coach-ing session; namely, bitterness and resentment for intruding or over directing the employee when he/she is very able and willing to act. The employee deserves some credit, and you need to know what is happening and how things will be improved or changed in a positive way.

Even good employees don't like to be misled. These peo-ple are perceptive; they know when you are being too cau-tious with them and avoiding sticky or unpleasant issues. We simply make the plea to deal with the issues openly, to clar-ify your intent to work in concert with them.

10

Finding a Coach

So far we have been focusing on when you need to give coaching to members of your team. But what about when you are a player, when there is a situation in which you would like some additional insight or ideas, or in which you feel awkward or unsure about what to do – when you need a sounding board, want feedback from someone who truly understands your situation, or where you would like to get a sanity check on whether you are focusing on the right issues?

In helping 50,000 leaders and managers become more effective coaches, we have found that all top performers attribute significant importance to the coaches they have encountered in their careers. These top performers initiate the contracts with their coaches: hiring, firing, and searching constantly for that coach who will give them the competitive edge. Using coaches is not limited to sports. Privately held businesses often seek outside members for their board of directors to bring fresh insights. As a matter of church law, the Pope has to have a spiritual advisor. The effectiveness of Alcoholics Anonymous is based not only on the climate of support and encouragement established in group meetings, but also on establishing a culture in which members are encouraged to seek out and work with "sponsors" who guide them, on a one-on-one basis, in actually implementing the steps of recovery. Some organizations have formalized a mentoring process for a select few high-potential employees. The mentor is usually not the person's immediate manager but someone who is knowledgeable about the norms of the

Coaches are not limited to sports

organization, knows the ropes, is successful in his or her own right, and is able to provide the gentle guidance, advice, and counsel necessary to help the high performers fulfill their capabilities.

Cultivate coaching relationships

We believe people who are concerned about learning and growth, regardless of their potential or talents, should seek out and retain the services of a coach. Coaching is no longer a top-down activity; it becomes each individual's responsibility to seek out and cultivate coaching relationships. Imagine the tremendous competitive advantage an organization would have if all the employees felt responsible for engaging and utilizing the services of a coach to help them learn and grow. Senge depicts the learning organization as "a community of inquiry and experimentation." Wouldn't it be refreshing if managers could ask employees, "What have you and your coach been learning that is of value to you, our team, and our department?" Consider the implications if this were true in our school systems. Students would actually assume responsibility for their learning. As Senge notes, the discipline of learning starts with dialogue. Argyris contends that learning occurs when we detect and correct errors. The implication is that learning is both internal and external with the help of others – in this case, *a coach*.

"Okay," you say, "I believe I can benefit from finding and utilizing a coach. Where do I start?"

WHAT DO YOU WANT FROM A COACH?

Where do I start?

What you are looking for is someone you can trust, who will help create a safe environment for learning – someone who will help solidify your thinking by asking probing questions and allowing you to ask probing questions. Your coach should focus on what you want or need to know. Look for someone who will share ideas, listen, and talk about your concerns.

Do self appraisal

You can't hire a "coach" in the abstract. You have to start by doing a self-appraisal so that you can identify prospective coaches who possess the necessary skills or insights. For work-related coaching, a good source for this appraisal would be your performance evaluation. Put aside questions or defense mechanisms regarding fairness or favoritism, and take the position, "Assuming this appraisal is accurate, what are the shortcomings or developmental needs that I can work on?" It might be developing a technical skill, resolving interpersonal problems like confronting poor performance by the people you supervise or listening attentively, improving personal habits like attention to detail, polishing sales techniques, or developing skills to meet changing needs.

With regard to outside-of-work matters, you might ask yourself questions like, "How could I be a better mother, or a better father, or a better church member, or a better son or daughter, or a better soccer coach? What would I like to know how to do that I've just never had anyone help me with?"

HOW MANY COACHES?

Instead of limiting yourself to one person who would need the skills to help you with everything on which you might like coaching, the objective should be to have a pool of coaches you can draw on to give you guidance in specific areas. The best sports teams have many specialty coaches: offensive coordinators, defensive coordinators, batting, pitching, quarterbacking. The list goes on. Why? Nobody should be expected to know everything. The prudent approach is to develop a network of coaches who have particular knowledge, insight, and experience that are useful to you. The more people you turn to for coaching, the better you will be able to triangulate their information and guidance with your own personal values. The more reliable coaches you nurture, the better your position to assess which ones to turn to for help and guidance.

Network of coaches

Some coaching may be very specific and short term in nature. I can recall asking a senior executive to critique a memo I was about to send to various executives introducing some needed changes in the performance appraisal system. Chosen because of his experience and political savvy, this coach gave me direct feedback that had a great impact. All he did was circle the number of times "I" appeared in the memo and attached a note, "Let's discuss." Although unintended, the overuse of "I" created a tone of self-importance in the memo. My good intentions could have been lost by the alienating effect of the overuse of "I." Blind to this until it was pointed out, I changed the memo which was then well received – a short, but critical lesson that has been recalled to this day.

DOES YOUR COACH PASS THE TEST?

Get a fresh idea

When you go looking for a coach, you are not looking for a clone of yourself – you've already got you. You are looking for someone who has experience or insight you don't have in dealing with a particular subject. A good coach can be found anywhere, in or outside of your present organization. Think about a specific coach, either one you have just started working with or one you are thinking about asking for coaching assistance. Your answers on the following ten-question quiz will determine if you have found the right coach for you.

Have you found the "right" coach?   Yes   No   ?

1. *The coach sees you as trustworthy, sincere, and wanting to learn.*

2. *The coach has a unique perspective or insight to offer.*

3. *The coach is willing to give of himself or herself and to help others.*

4. *The coach is easy to talk to and can be trusted. You do not feel vulnerable.*

5. *The coach wants to see you succeed.*

6. *The coach is a teacher, willing to help others grow and develop.*

7. *The coach expects to learn something during your time together.*

8. *The coach believes that you should grow out of the need for his/her help and would never use phrases like "You need me" or "I can help you get ahead."*

9. *The coach believes that you need to struggle and find your own way and would never say: "I know best."*

10. *You have a good feeling about working with this coach.*

Total

Scoring: If you have 10 YES's, you've found the perfect coach. Are there any perfect 10's? We know there are. Keep looking if you have checked any NO's or ?'s for your particular coach. Consider the following.

Your credibility. The coach has to believe in you, to be convinced that you are sincere, want to learn, and can be trusted. Your credibility is all you can offer in return for the coach's time and energy. Generally, this credibility comes from the coach having seen you in operation; you are not strangers. The coach considers you trustworthy; you have supported him or her in the past. Question 1.

The coach's credibility. Coaches cannot be of value unless they have a unique perspective and are willing to help. Although difficult, check out the coaches' track record in helping others. Do they give of themselves? Do they value helping others? Do others find them easy to talk to? Do others value their perspective? Do you value their perspective? Can they be trusted? Questions 2 through 4.

Check track record

A desire to see you succeed. A crucial distinction between your coach and other acquaintances is that the coach wants to see you succeed – not necessarily to advance or achieve monetary goals, but to achieve your potential, to be the best you can be. The ultimate payoff is that the coach will feel good about your success. Question 5.

The coach as teacher. We don't mean by profession. The issue is, does the coach enjoy seeing others grow and develop? Is he/she secure enough to be challenged? Good coaches don't create dependency relationships. They are happy when you can fly on your own. "You need me" and "I can help you get ahead" create unhealthy dependency/reciprocal relationships.

Does the coach have the patience to allow you to discover both the questions and the answers, or do you sense a need to always provide answers and tell others what to do?

One of the authors said, "When first starting out in my career, I felt comfortable going to a wise manager for advice. Rather than explore the nature of my questions or help me to think things through he would always have a ready answer. At first this was comforting, until I discovered that I was doing things the way he would, not thinking for myself. Did I have convictions, beliefs, ideas? Yes, but this coach was not forcing me to develop them. My reliance on and relationship with this coach ended." Questions 6 through 9.

Your feelings. As a final test, trust your instincts. Does it feel right to work with this person? If you are uncertain about a potential coach, trust those uneasy feelings. If the information and guidance the coach is providing feels wrong, re-evaluate the coach. If you are uncomfortable with the guidance, you're not talking to the right coach. Question 10.

OTHERS WHO ARE "HELPFUL" BUT MIGHT NOT PASS THE TEST

The friend. Liking someone clearly makes coaching more enjoyable, but this is not a sufficient condition. To provide you with helpful guidance requires more than just friendship. A friend's trust in you is the first but just one of the five criteria of a good coaching candidate. A friend is not impartial and finds it hard to provide the positive and negative feedback that is such a critical part of the coaching relationship.

Coaches need to provide reliable information

The meddler. The coach doesn't provide just advice or hearsay information but provides reliable information and a perspective that is both unique and useful. However, the usefulness must extend to helping you achieve your self-interest. The meddler cannot meet these two conditions.

Your boss. Ideally, this person should be your head coach, but this is not always the case. If your manager actively provides you with the coaching assistance you need, great! If not, don't wait; take the initiative and find those coaches who can help you. Don't expect your boss to be the coach for all seasons. An interesting experiment would be to share with your boss the way these coaches have helped you to learn and grow. Who knows, by example, this experience may help your boss become an even better coach for you and the other employees he/she supervises. The message to remember is that just because your immediate boss doesn't, or won't, provide you the coaching help you need, you are not cut off from seeking other alternatives for this help with your growth and development.

Contracting with Your Coach(es)

Unless you have a coach, you may well approach coaching with an air of superiority that will detract from your ability to be a coach. If you think being coached is a sign of weakness, that attitude will infect the coaching relationship, and some of what you might be seeking to transmit will be filtered out. If you really believe in coaching, articulate the contract.

Believe in coaching

A sincere request for coaching is flattering, and many people will cheerfully offer their insight if asked in a way that makes it clear that you will not abuse their time or their confidence. Although your contract is informal, a number of things need to be articulated, understood, and agreed to by you and your coach.

The terms. In real life, few coaches get lifetime contracts. Even though you are looking for long-term relationships, don't put yourself in a position where a coach's feelings will be hurt and support will turn to resentment if you stop asking for coaching or have to reject the advice. Be clear and realistic on the help and the time you are asking for. Our recommendation is to ask for a trial period of three to six months, then reevaluate if both parties still feel it is a win-win relationship. Since you are asking for very specific help, not coaching on everything, you should be able to keep your requests on the other person's time to a reasonable level. Ideally, you will interact with many coaches over the course of your career. What are you prepared to give? This will be a two-way street, requiring some creativity to return some value for the coach's time and effort.

The focus. The coach should not only know what specific areas you are seeking help in but should feel free to say no. Although the request for help is flattering, the option to not become your coach should always exist without any feelings of guilt. Be specific with your requests.

The ground rules. You will need to make your preferred way of being coached explicit. How do you learn new things? Through experimentation, reading, reflections? You want advice and insight, but you also want to make the final decision on accepting this advice. You are not asking the coach to do your job for you, just to provide a unique perspective for you to consider in your decision-making process. Don't seek advice you don't plan to consider seriously. Don't waste people's time if you don't intend to listen fully to what is said and to supply valid reasons for not following the advice.

Consider advice seriously

Fuel
the
fire

What you are offering. Without genuine consideration, the contract is one way. Be explicit about your commitment to learn, work, try, and experiment. Don't assume that your coach understands your commitment. Your excitement and energy will add fuel to the coaching fire.

What will make your coach look forward to your meetings? Try this experiment. Ask any volunteer athletic coach what players are the most rewarding to work with. The authors having coached youth soccer for numerous age groups would answer, "The ones with the right attitude." Sure, the athletically gifted are fun but they have natural, God-given talents. We were glad we had the chance to work with these players. However, the most rewarding were those who loved practice, wanted to constantly improve, and made us stretch to develop unique ways of teaching and coaching to keep it interesting. Upon reflection they, not the won-loss record, are why we coached.

How will it end. You need to define how you will know when the coaching relationship has run a reasonable course. Either party should have the right to end the relationship and feel good about it. Our advice is to set up specific evaluation dates every six months to ask, "Are we both still getting value out of this relationship and should we continue?"

THE ONLY REMAINING STUMBLING BLOCK

Ask
for
help

If you've honestly assessed your strengths and areas where you could use some coaching help, thought through a list of candidates and narrowed it down to those you think could be good coaches for you, the only thing remaining is to ask for their help. This may be the hardest part of the entire process. The only one who can take this step is you. The first attempt will be the hardest, but the benefits of supportive coaching and help from a valued other will far outweigh your initial uneasiness about establishing this contact. Even though it feels unnatural, our best advice comes from a well-known shoe advertising slogan – Just do it!

Just do it!

11

Coaching at the Executive Level

The higher you climb the ladder in this organization, the less chance you have of getting feedback about your performance. The working rule of thumb is "the farther up you go, the stranger things get," especially in the way you are reviewed and rewarded. . . .We seem to have time for everything else, but not time to give our top people the kind of reviews they need to help them develop.
— Executive-level controller

WHY COACHING SHOULD INCLUDE EXECUTIVES

Executives by the nature of their work (unstructured, uncertain, and ill-defined) could benefit from coaching discussions with those in a position to observe both the results produced as well as the behaviors exhibited. However, most senior executives view their primary roles as protecting and enhancing shareholder's values, establishing corporate strategy, and avoiding litigation, bankruptcy, and prosecution. Coaching peers and associates isn't in their job descriptions. Few executives fail because they lack technical skills or motivation. In a classic study by the Center for Creative Leadership (CCL), four enduring themes for why executives derail are present over time and across countries[1]:

Four themes

- *problems with interpersonal relationships*
- *failure to meet business objectives*
- *failure to build and lead a team*
- *inability to change or adapt during a transition.*

These four cry out for the personal attention of a coach. Why is it that organizations and executives take a sink-or-swim philosophy with such a valuable resource pool?

SIX MYTHS RELATIVE TO EXECUTIVE COACHING

On the basis of in-depth interviews with 84 executives from 11 major organizations in manufacturing and service industries, Longenecker and Gioia[2] uncovered six myths relative to executive appraisals. Although their focus is limited to performance appraisals, their findings have some interesting implications for day-to-day coaching of executives.

Myth #1 Executives neither need nor want structured performance reviews.

Every executive interviewed dismissed this common belief and said that systematic feedback in some form was crucial. It is amazing that those in the most influential positions are left to sink or swim. This would seem to be a high-cost gamble and one that would contribute to the failure of good people. One CEO of a Fortune 500 company contracted with us to gather 360-degree feedback from his direct reports. When asked why he wanted this information, he responded, "I have moved around so fast that I was never in a position long enough to get any feedback about my strengths and weaknesses. I believe this myopic view of the world is dangerous and both value this type of feedback and want to send a message to the other executives that we should be availing ourselves of this valuable information."

Myth #2 A formal review is beneath the dignity of an executive.

The outdated notion that the formal review is a demeaning and aversive experience may lead to the conclusion that executive status carries with it the rite of passage to not have to endure this indignity. The central focus of our coaching model is a partnership relationship built on support and trust. This produces a positive discussion between people that is aimed at improving and maintaining performance, growth, and personal satisfaction. It would be interesting to conjecture what difference, if any, replacing the word coach with teacher or mentor might have on executives who feel this is below their dignity.

Myth #3: Top-level executives are too busy to conduct appraisals.

Myth #1 (margin note)

Myth #2 (margin note)

Myth #3 (margin note)

Unfortunately this "excuse" is not limited to executives. If you don't believe a critical responsibility is to coach those you work with, then it is natural to view this as a low priority. A quote from one of the executives interviewed seems to be a perfect response: "It seems like we have time for lots of things that are a lot less important than talking about enhancing performance and executive development. There should always be time for a process that contributes to higher performance and productivity, and paradoxically, the saving of time."

Myth #4: A lack of feedback fosters autonomy and creativity in executives.

Myth #4

This strong-individualism view of forcing people to figure things out for themselves may have been effective in the past. The need for more teamwork requires a shared understanding of the organization's vision and mission, and this demands more, not less, information. Lack of information breeds doubt and frustration; it allows little problems to fester into big ones and opportunities to be lost.

Myth #5: Results are the only basis for assessing executive performance.

Myth #5

Executives can benefit as much if not more from coaching on how they produce the results. People can make their numbers at the expense of the company, associates, and other departments. Issues like communications, team building, quality, mentoring, and how they are coaching their associates are valuable areas for discussion. In the CCL study, three out of four reasons for derailment dealt with management style and behavior, not with making their numbers. As one executive stated: "Sure, you have to get results; that's why we're in business. But, you also need to look at the road you took to get the results. You need feedback on process and style and the intangibles that you can't quantify. The hell of the matter is that the results evaluation is easy; it's also a cop-out."

Myth #6: Evaluation of executive performance simply cannot be captured via formal performance appraisal.

Myth #6

Without question high-performing executives have a lot of intuition, ambiguity, gut feelings, flashes of insight, and other non-measurable attributes. Like leadership, executive performance may be subject to what one of our client feels: "I can't tell you what makes a good leader, but I know one when I see one." Feedback and coaching on executive performance may differ in character, not in principle: a supportive relationship, open discussion on performance expectations, continual discussion about performance, and a collaborative approach to solve problems and define new opportunities.

The executives interviewed wanted ongoing, specific feedback beyond a nominal yearly review. Instead they were receiving a steady diet of executive-style feedback, either none at all or that which was too general to be useful. An effective executive should be treated as a rare commodity, one that needs to be nurtured by an executive coach. We feel that ignoring this coaching role in the executive ranks is a tremendous waste of talent.

Do executives resist coaching? Similar results were found in a recent survey of consultants and upper-level executives that asked, "Do you see evidence that executives resist the coaching role?" Ninety percent said yes. The reasons fell into three categories[3]:

Skills. "I'm uncomfortable with coaching." "I don't know how to coach."

Role conflict. "I have too many other demands on my time. Development's not my job."

Values. "They should be able to figure things out for themselves."

One of the executives interviewed by Longnecker and Gioia best summed up our position on a more aggressive approach to executive coaching: "Many of us at the top are guilty of not focusing on what we are trying to do and how we are trying to do it. We don't plan for our executives' performance, and we don't give or get regular feedback. We seem to ignore the people in the organization who could do the most with good personal performance information. In doing so, we perpetually make trouble for ourselves, and I really don't know why."

WHAT WOULD MAKE EXECUTIVES WANT TO COACH?

The simple answer is if their compensation were tied to their coaching performance. Our fear is that this would mandate the activity and not guarantee quality coaching interactions between executives and others. Our preference would be to make coaching easier and worthwhile for exec-

utives by providing one-on-one help in how to coach. We
are suggesting a coaching-the-coach relationship similar to
the one-on-one help executives receive in public speaking,
press relations, financial matters, or other skills that are not
automatic. A coaching-the-coach approach can help executives in fulfilling the coaching role, instead of just adding a
new item to their job descriptions.

Coaching-the-coach

The coach can be someone from HR, as long as he or she
doesn't take on the actual coaching responsibilities; a peer;
or an external person. Although not exclusive, here are types
of help this coach can provide the executive:

- *Undertake a confidential review of each of the executive's direct reports to ascertain their strengths, weaknesses, and potential.*

- *Gather feedback from the executive's direct reports about
his/her/their leadership strengths and weaknesses.*

- *Observe actual coaching discussions or team meetings,
provide the executive feedback, and help develop
improvement plans.*

- *Provide information and short skill-building sessions on
such topics as the role of the coach, active listening, and
handling difficult employees.*

- *Role play a challenging conversation that the executive is
facing.*

- *Be a sounding board for ideas the executive has for helping others.*

Through reorganization, a division president inherited a
team of people that he neither had selected nor worked with
in the past. He was frustrated that they were not working as
a team. So we first discussed his definition and criteria for an
effective team. Second, we interviewed all the team members, discovering that they felt they operated as an effective
team but that one member was seen as particularly disruptive to the team's efforts. The president realized that until
something was done with this one member, any other efforts
at building the entire team would be futile. His first
response was that he had the latitude to replace anyone who
didn't fit with his style. Our counsel was that although this
was always an option, a heart-to-heart coaching discussion

to clarify expectations might be a productive first step. The president agreed, and we discussed his approach for this discussion and offered specific alternatives. Over the next month, three coaching discussions were held. After each we replayed it with the president and helped with constructive suggestions and alternatives. After the last discussion the president was convinced that the person was committed to change her disruptive behavior and become an active team player. Would this change have occurred and a valuable resource been retained without a coach for the coach? Possibly. The coach for the coach made it easier for the president to fulfill his coaching responsibilities and gain a valuable ally for developing the executive team to lead the entire organization. Making coaching easier and worthwhile for executives is what coaching-the-coach is all about.

1 Ellen Van Velsor and Jean Brittain Leslie. Why Executives Derail: Perspectives Across Time and Cultures. *Academy of Management Executive,* 1995 Vol. 9 No. 4. pp. 62-72.

2 Clinton O. Longenecker and Dennis A. Gioia. The Executive Appraisal Paradox. *Academy of Management Executive,* 1992 Vol. 6 No. 2. pp. 18-28.

3 Lynda McDermott. Wanted: Chief Executive Coach. *Training & Development.* May 1996, pp. 67-70.

12

Concluding Thoughts

HOW PEOPLE CHANGE

Coaching is a process of helping employees experience and work through the three key stages of change. However, employees don't always need manager assistance in order to change, develop, or improve. Often, the employee is perfectly capable of navigating through the key stages of change that result in new behavior patterns and attitudes. For leaders, this represents both good and bad news. The good news is that you will find very few employees who need constant coaching, and the bad news is that you may not be needed as often or as much as you might think.

3 phases of coaching

On the basis of our research, we want to describe how people change in organizational and job settings and how the leader can initiate and support the change process when there is a need. (see Table 12.1.)

In the first stage of the change process, the employee is either unaware that change will be useful, or the employee is content with his/her behavior and attitudes. In this stage, the leader is beginning to observe and notice definite signs or early warning signals. With a little time, these observations become more unsettling. Ultimately, a decision is reached to either confront the issues or ignore them, live with the pain, and take heavy doses of organizational aspirin; i.e., try to forget it, quit noticing, or rationalize that it really isn't that bad.

First stage

The process of guided change moves to Stage 2 when the leader decides to confront the problem and/or the employee doesn't show any signs of self-adjustment. In this stage, it is

Second stage

vital that the leader be clear on his/her role. It is easy to adopt a position that, "Hey I'm the boss here. When I tell someone to jump, they better say 'How high?'" Sorry, this isn't the Marine Corps, and you can't make people change any more than you can make someone be motivated to do a job.

The leader as a catalyst

The leader best serves as a catalyst. This means you can initiate and draw attention to issues. You can help mobilize the forces and ingredients that in turn support and heighten the employee's felt need for change, and you can help navigate and adjust the speed of the process. However, the employee will ultimately make a decision to assimilate or resist change. In the Western industrial society, workers should have this freedom.

The leader needs to help facilitate and add clarity when the decisions are tough and unclear for the employee. Ultimately, employees may be trying to tell you that they are not matched well with the requirements of the job, or that they are in an incompatible relationship. In either case, they may be having difficulty putting this into words. You need to help them explore all the options, even the difficult ones like separation.

Adhere to the eight steps

Surprise, our recommendation for the leader's role in Stage 2 is to adhere to the eight steps as a template for initiating, mobilizing, and guiding this task. Our belief is that if you trust this process, it will work. Stage 2 is the main event for the employees. This is where they come to grips with the issues. Once these issues are laid out, there is usually an initial reaction of denial, excuses, and/or some anger. As the concern is developed, employees will experience tension and readiness for change through introspection and self-analysis. The process presents an excellent opportunity to redirect employees to a commitment, new goals, and action plans. It can also create a need to reexamine their current level of satisfaction with social relationships, job structure, and career match.

Third stage

After orchestrating Stage 2 the leader needs to figure out how to best support the events and activities of Stage 3. Like learning to play a new sport or a musical instrument, Stage 3 requires some risk taking and a willingness to expose yourself and to be a novice. You need to remain hopeful even though you may feel awkward, uneasy, and self conscious.

The leader plays a vital role in follow-up by providing encouragement, consultation, and tangible help if needed. Once the employee feels a little validation and reward from these initial awkward steps, the new behaviors or attitudes become self-sustaining. The employee begins to feel better, self-esteem rises, and a new state of equilibrium or comfort sets in. This doesn't happen overnight; it takes patience and courage from the leader. You need to give the employee a chance to try, experiment, and fail, if necessary. There has to be some maneuvering room to test and to show room for improvement. Often, there is a decline before there is strong detectable improvement.

Contentment	Renewal
Denial	Confusion

Claes Janssen

Employees need the chance to try, experiment, fail if necessary.

Our model of guided change gives leaders strong clues about the role they need to play in the three stages. We can't guarantee fast progress through each stage. We will promise that if you stick with it, your chances of having lasting and deep improvement will increase. *See Table 12.1 on page 152.*

10 BASIC COACHING VALUES

As a result of studying and observing leaders engaged in the coaching process, we have developed a set of basic values inherent in the coaching model. If you have captured the vision of the coaching process, these values will not come as a big surprise. We believe they are worth stating in the hope that more leaders will adopt and assimilate them, and that their behavior and actions will be consistent with these values:

1. Every employee can benefit from having access (via coaching) to a leader's wisdom, experience, and unique perspective, regardless of whether coaching involves tough problems, concerns, or positive opportunities for the employee.

Coaching is beneficial

2. Clarity and candor between a leader and employee are fundamental to building trust and respect.

Clarity & candor

3. Employee involvement and ownership in developing solutions are vital to the coaching process.

Involvement

4. Patience, planning, and deliberation, without procrastination, are critical to effective coaching.

Patience

5. Coaching implies a strong, forward-looking, action orientation rather than a focus on the past (mistakes, excuses, over-analysis, and fault-finding).

Forward-looking

Table 12.1

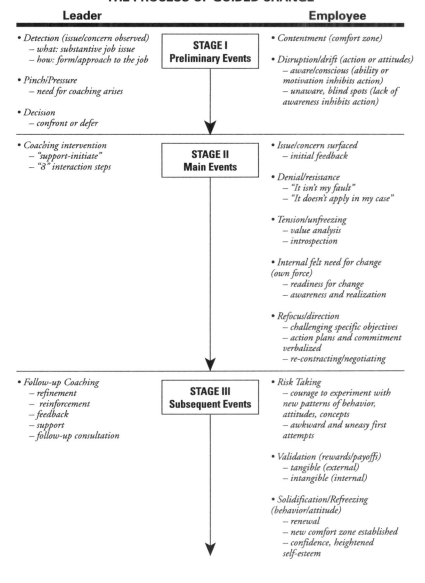

3 STAGES OF CHANGE
THE PROCESS OF GUIDED CHANGE

Leader		Employee
• *Detection (issue/concern observed)* *– what: substantive job issue* *– how: form/approach to the job* • *Pinch/Pressure* *– need for coaching arises* • *Decision* *– confront or defer*	**STAGE I** **Preliminary Events**	• *Contentment (comfort zone)* • *Disruption/drift (action or attitudes)* *– aware/conscious (ability or motivation inhibits action)* *– unaware, blind spots (lack of awareness inhibits action)*
• *Coaching intervention* *– "support-initiate"* *– "3" interaction steps*	**STAGE II** **Main Events**	• *Issue/concern surfaced* *– initial feedback* • *Denial/resistance* *– "It isn't my fault"* *– "It doesn't apply in my case"* • *Tension/unfreezing* *– value analysis* *– introspection* • *Internal felt need for change (own force)* *– readiness for change* *– awareness and realization* • *Refocus/direction* *– challenging specific objectives* *– action plans and commitment verbalized* *– re-contracting/negotiating*
• *Follow-up Coaching* *– refinement* *– reinforcement* *– feedback* *– support* *– follow-up consultation*	**STAGE III** **Subsequent Events**	• *Risk Taking* *– courage to experiment with new patterns of behavior, attitudes, concepts* *– awkward and uneasy first attempts* • *Validation (rewards/payoffs)* *– tangible (external)* *– intangible (internal)* • *Solidification/Refreezing (behavior/attitude)* *– renewal* *– new comfort zone established* *– confidence, heightened self-esteem*

6. Supportiveness is the most important ingredient in gaining lasting employee cooperation. There is no substitute for meaningful and serious leader/employee partnerships.

Supportiveness

7. Coaching requires courage and risk taking. It is never as easy and simple as we would like. Leaders will always feel some doubt and apprehension.

Courage and risk taking

8. Leaders and events play contributing roles in concerns and challenges facing employees. It isn't healthy to deny these roles. Leaders need to model ownership of their piece of the problem.

Mutual responsibility

9. Coaching and negotiation aren't always the solution, but they should be faithfully exhausted before moving on to other management alternatives (i.e., discipline, punishment, separation, etc.).

Coaching isn't the only answer

10. Finally, you need to trust the process and attend to the skills and business of coaching that have been outlined in this book. When you neglect or overlook an element, you cut down on your chance of success.

Trust the process

IT'S NOT WHAT YOU THINK, COACH, IT'S WHAT YOU DO

If you are like the leader or employees in our study, you would have little difficulty describing the elements in an effective coaching session. Even ineffective leaders could correctly define what should occur. The difference was that the ineffective leader was inhibited or could not apply or enact the desired behaviors when asked to do so in a real-time coaching session. The effective leaders, on the other hand, were able to apply the desired behaviors.

It's all in the doing

What causes the discrepancy between knowing what to do and actually doing it? Our best guess is that most managers have the knowledge because they have been exposed to a wide number of good coaching models, both in an organizational setting and off the job – a teacher, minister, friend, professional counselor, etc. Add to this the constant flow of information and literature on effective people skills for leaders. Leaders are also employees, and they know how they would want to be treated by their boss in a coaching session. When you add all of this up, it is not surprising that leaders have adequate sources of information to formulate an accurate mental picture of quality coaching.

The mystery is why the discrepancy occurs between

descriptions and actions. One possibility is that, for some, their tough business philosophy of how leaders should actually relate to employees is in conflict with the notions of openly exhibiting supportive behavior, seeking employee input, sharing responsibilities for problem solving, etc. The group's values and attitudes about how a manager should relate to an employee gets in the way of being an effective coach. Freeing up to apply the positive concepts that they already know requires that they allow themselves to experience the benefits first-hand and to see that most employees will not take advantage of them. A behavioral change can come about only after experimentation with, and testing of, the impact of the new set of highly beneficial leader behaviors. Furthermore, leaders need opportunities for extensive practice in order to become efficient and to convert mental images of coaching into a reality. In a training session, time needs to be devoted to multiple practice sessions in which this experimentation and testing can occur.

You need opportunities to practice

A second possibility for this discrepancy is that some leaders truly believe that their behavior is consistent with their descriptions of an effective coaching session. They perceive no difference between what they say and what they do, even though employees would dispute this. Their problem is more difficult because the managers' perceptions belie the reality of what they actually do as a coach. These managers respond to a presentation of the coaching model described in this text with nods of support. They complain that other managers are incapable of following the model, as they do with their employees. To increase these managers' coaching effectiveness requires their first seeing the difference between what they say and do, then describing what those specific inconsistent behaviors are and the agony they create for the employee. Again, training time needs to be devoted to providing the managers with candid feedback about their behavior and specific alternative behaviors to experiment with during future practice sessions.

You know what is needed!

Our conclusion is that managers know what is needed in an effective coaching session. Other than a brief overview and review, we do not need to spend valuable training time telling managers to be more participative, or explaining what an effective coaching session entails. We need to spend our time allowing managers to experience the benefits of an effective coaching model and discussing the obstacles to using this model. Second, in providing feedback on their coaching behavior, we need to devote heavy doses of training time to multiple practice and discussion sessions that explore the rewards of good coaching. Our belief and promise is that, if you persist, you will grow increasingly comfortable with the 8-Step Coaching Model and will adapt and incorporate the skills into your own unique style.

THE ART OF COACHING
(Be Assertive, Be Realistic, and Trust the Process)

ART

Leaders constantly ask us how to be better coaches. Much to their surprise, the answer is short and simple: Be assertive, be realistic, and trust the process. A coach can be helpful to the employee by clearly and directly stating concerns and dealing with important issues; being realistic with expectations, plans, feedback, consequences, and commitments; and trusting the coaching process outlined in this book.

The employee will produce, grow, and become more supportive only if the leader can bring together and orchestrate, in a positive way, the employee's knowledge, skills, abilities, and willingness to achieve. Leaders don't create this critical mass. The best they can do is highlight, clarify, and serve as a catalyst. The coaching process does work if the employee or manager allows it to by patiently persisting with the skills and knowledge outlined in this book.

Serve as a catalyst

If the employee has made up his/her mind not to change, about the only thing you can try is the ancient art of hypnosis, or else wait until a miracle drug is approved by the Food and Drug Administration. If you will trust the process and pay serious attention to planning, execution of the 8 Steps, and follow-up, you will see some progress. But, if it doesn't come early or quickly, please don't abandon the process. A lot of leaders turn back and resort to more drastic measures just when they are on the verge of some progress.

REGULAR TTA SESSIONS
(Talk, Think, and Act)

TTA

This is really the essence of Step 8 in the coaching model...regular frequent contact. Contact and follow-up

Frequent contact

are not born out of the need to be snoopy or over-controlling, nor are they an expression of your mistrust of the employee. Rather they arise from the need to be supportive, interested, involved, and committed, as well as from the need to see results.

At times, when the question comes up (and it does invariably) of how much coaching is enough, the response has been a bit controversial. The hard data on this question suggest ideally once per week (or once every two weeks at the least) if you really hope to gain the benefits of a TTA session. For some leaders with many employees (10 or more reporting directly) or for leaders supervising employees with low job task variety or impact, it may be that a monthly TTA session would be very workable. But, frankly, that is as much as we will compromise on answering this tough question. Many managers react quickly and say there are so many other things to do: "I can't afford to spend that much time with employees." Our response is, "You're right. . .managers will always be busy, and if you believe you are a leader, as well as a manager, then you can't afford not to spend 30-40 minutes in a one-to-one TTA session once each week or two."

Once a week

The next question or concern that invariably comes up is, "What if there is a lack of issues or concerns to talk about?" We are tempted to say, "Open your eyes," but that seems a bit curt! Nevertheless, our basic concerns are that you are not attending to leadership, not delegating enough, not fully utilizing the employee, and not giving enough permission to take some risks or be more expressive. It is you, the leader, who is paying a big price if you are not magnifying your efforts through others or getting the full leverage intended by having employees report to you. If there are no specific concerns or issues, then you can use the meeting time to gather information as an update on progress, do some developmental or motivational coaching, pass along information, etc. As leader, you can also ask for feedback, model a positive response to these issues, and show the employee that you are concerned and interested in being an effective partner. Once you have done these things, then give yourself and the employee a break and call the meeting short. In fact, doing this once in a while is good so employees maintain some freshness and so you respond authentically to the fact that nothing important is happening.

Remember, the important message that you are sending is that this employee and his/her job are as important as budgets, monthly reports, staff meetings, and all the other bureaucratic BS that all leaders and managers have to put up with. We know some initiative on your part will have to be taken to make employees feel important, number one, and to dedicate the time on a regularly scheduled basis (i.e., every other Wednesday) to connect with your employees. We simply find that a lot of organizations either don't want to or don't know how to get leaders to make the employees feel like valued partners and to maintain effective accountability. The system we are proposing is simple, and it takes only a little time. The best way to start is to circulate a memo or post a note that you would like to meet individually with your employees (direct reports) more often and that you have set aside a certain time during the week or month. Once people begin coming in, you can say more about the purpose and intent of the TTA sessions.

Dedicate a certain time

COACHING VS. PERFORMANCE APPRAISAL

The question often comes up, "Isn't coaching a lot like the familiar performance appraisal process?" Our answer is that it is dramatically different. We originally became interested in the coaching process because of our experiences with the deficiencies of performance appraisal. We had been asked to devise a customized performance appraisal system, along with a training program, for a Fortune 500 corporation. After working through the resistance that naturally accompanies adoption of a massive program such as this, we noticed one consistent piece of feedback coming from managers at all levels. That message was, "Give us some help, ideas, and training on how to manage an employee's performance from day to day, from one concern to the next." These managers grew to accept the performance appraisal process, but they felt that an annual or series of annual performance reviews wasn't the answer to improving employee performance and maximizing cooperation. Something less formal and more flexible was needed to use with employees on a more frequent basis. So we began our preliminary research and data gathering to construct a coaching model or tool to address this very appropriate objection to perfor-

"If it looks and smells like a rose, why do we keep calling it a carnation?"

mance appraisal as the primary management tool for human resources.

Because of this experience, we spend considerable time delineating and defining the differences between these two processes. Table 12.2 thoroughly differentiates the two methods. We hope it will reduce confusion and ambiguity and be useful for those who may be interested in using both processes in their organizations.

BEYOND COACHING:
When Things Are Getting Out of Control

What if the employee doesn't respond?

Leaders often ask us, "What do you do when you have tried to coach and counsel an employee about a performance concern, and the employee has not responded?" Unfortunately, we see far too many cases where the leader hasn't, in good faith, tried to coach the employee or to put the leader's concerns into words. Often, leaders look for a quick fix alternative to what is perceived as a difficult and painful confrontation. We have also learned from first-hand experience that coaching is usually not a one-shot effort. It may take regular ongoing discussions and experiences to achieve the level of support and cooperation needed.

When you have truly exhausted your good-faith efforts to coach the employee into a change, you have the right to move to the next best alternative, to a coaching-based solution. In certain situations, the employee simply may not appreciate or value the coaching approach. In organizations today, many employees have grown accustomed to and dependent on heavy authority in the work place, or they just don't feel attached to the job or organization. We are not advocating that the leader wait for someone to pass out a permission slip to try a different approach; rather, the leader should tell the employee that the coaching approach hasn't worked and that it is time to take a different path.

Other alternatives

Probably the best thing a leader can do is literally call time out, pull back, and reexamine the entire interpersonal/working contract or agreement with the employee. The leader needs to reconsider the basic assumptions and understanding about the employee's role and terms of employment in the organization. This is a major renegotiation effort. It is very possible that the job demands or personal expectations

Table 12.2

COACHING	PERFORMANCE APPRAISAL
Definition	
Interpersonal influence, exercised by a leader in specific situations or in response to critical incidents or development opportunities, designed to attain a specific goal or planned change in behavior or attitude. Integrative and interactive communication, dialogue, and exchange are used to gain employee's support for new direction and change.	*Formal and more general feedback and information at predetermined intervals designed to apprise employees of the leader's perception of job effort and success. To let employees know how they are doing and their relative value to the organization.*
Goals/Outcomes	
To take immediate and full advantage of development opportunities as they occur. To have the employee understand and accept changes that will increase their effectiveness. To eliminate obstacles and impediments to better performance.	*To provide information for management decision making (rewards, compensation, discipline, promotions, training, succession planning, etc.). To reinforce desired behaviors and objectively evaluate performance over time. To close the books on past performance and plan new goals for the coming year.*
Time Focus	
Frequent, as a spontaneous reaction to inadequate behavior or attitudes, or as a regular planned and deliberate "time out." Emphasis on current events, here-and-now concerns and opportunities.	*Less frequent (usually annual or semi-annual), conducted at the beginning or end of a year or business cycle rather than when work is in progress. Focus on the past and what was or wasn't done.*
Leader's Task	
• *To confront specific situations or incidents where employee behavior is less than expected or where there is an opportunity for development or learning.* • *To pose a problem, seek resolution and commitment, integrate ideas, and make agreements and plans.*	• *To document and evaluate overall strengths and weaknesses.* • *To review agreements and job responsibilities and to compare against predetermined objectives.* • *To document the employee's value and contribution to the company and submit performance reports.* • *To integrate the objectives of the work group and the individual.*
Values	
Coaching provides an opportunity for the leader to act out and communicate these values: • *That it is better to catch problems before they become unmanageable.* • *That it is wise to aim for modest improvements rather than expect giant changes all at once.* • *That employees need adequate time to assimilate and demonstrate progress.* • *That employees need to accept responsibility for change.* • *That the best results are achieved with a forward-looking/action orientation.*	*The performance appraisal process seems to value:* • *General and overall feedback.* • *Clear documentation and record keeping.* • *Quantity of topics discussed rather than quality resolutions pertaining to individual events.* • *A certain amount of secrecy around results and ratings.* • *Decision making (promotion, salary, training, rather than behavior/attitude change.*

and objectives of the employee or leader have changed suffi-
ciently that a real pressure point has been created in the
leader/employee relationship. Remember, a social contract
between a leader and employee works as long as there is
"mutual consent and valid consideration" for both parties. If
a new agreement and a shared vision of common goals can
be reached, then a new state of leader/employee stability and
equilibrium will be achieved. If not, the leader and employee should begin to explore and plan a way to separate effectively. Some leaders say they can't get along without the
employee. No problem – you simply need to look for creative ways to restructure the employee's job or reassign or
retrain the employee to cut your losses and limit your exposure. You may consider "down-sizing" the employee's role to
fit the needs of the situation.

Disciplinary action

Another strategy is to pursue a path or formal disciplinary
or probationary action. Obviously this is riskier; it may be a
path of no return in the sense that cultivating a healthy relationship in a climate of hostility and possible resentment,
anger, and embarrassment over disciplinary action is difficult. You may be forced to pursue this path to the unpleasant end of a separation, the ultimate challenge for any leader.
The other thing you may consider is to take two aspirin, grin
and bear it, and go on lots of short vacations.

IT WORKS IN GROUPS

How many times have you sat in meetings and had these
thoughts:

What are we talking about that for?
What's the point of this discussion?
We're really getting off track now.
*I don't think they know exactly what they are going to
do as a result of this meeting.*
Why make such a big deal over this issue anyway?

Not another meeting

How to use the eight steps

Having facilitated meetings, we often make the same kind
of observations, and we see a lot of wasted time due to poor
meeting management. Managers can hold better meetings
by using the Eight Step Coaching Model as a guideline,

especially if it is a problem solving meeting.

With a little modification the eight steps can be used to improve your next meeting.

Step One – Be Supportive: As in the coaching session the meeting leader needs to show support throughout the meeting. This can be done by:

> *Encouraging the open expression of differences, disagreements, or objections in a way that is not punishing to the person.*
>
> *Listening to others' points of view.*
>
> *Accepting some responsibility for the current situation and the issue being discussed.*
>
> *Being collaborative/flexible in defining and solving the problem.*
>
> *Keeping the exchange objective and positive versus subjective, personal, or negative.*

There is also a place, at the start of the meeting, to state your intentions and ground rules for the meeting that indicate your willingness to be supportive and collaborative during the meeting.

Step Two – Define the Topic and Needs: The leader can help the group crystallize the definition of the situation or opportunities. Write this out on a flip chart, or try to make things as visible as possible. Discuss fully the perceptions of everyone. A consensus on the situation or opportunity can serve as the focal point for all future discussion.

After the definition phase, the members may want to clarify each other's wants or needs regarding the situation. The idea is not to get a master list but to define the similarities and unique differences among the meeting participants. This is an important activity; don't hurry past this step.

Step Three – Establish Impact: The group needs to decide whether the current situation or future opportunity is worth doing something about.

The meeting leader needs to make sure every member has an opportunity to state, agree, or disagree with the list of positive or negative impacts of the current situation. A good question to keep asking the group is, "What effect is this situation having on us?"

Step One

Step Two

Step Three

Ideas should be captured on a flip chart. In this way, the meeting leader is building a case and has some written support for doing something different. By clarifying the impact, the group is building its own motivation for looking at a new direction.

Step Four

Step Four – Initiate a Plan: The lessons learned, while working with an individual during a coaching session, apply directly to groups. Ultimately, the leader wants to know who will do what, when, where, and how.

In meetings, a lot of good discussion will occur, but the action plans are often left vague or the responsibility for implementation is assumed. We suggest that these actions be documented on a flip chart or that each person write the meeting leader a memo outlining what he/she committed to do as a result of this meeting.

Step Five

Step Five – Get A Commitment: This step is simple but is avoided in meetings as much as it is in the individual coaching process. You need to be direct and ask members who are responsible for specific action plans if they are willing to try them. Tie it together, and open the discussion for possible reasons why the agreed-to plans can't be accomplished. Better to know now, than later, if problems and resistance have set in.

Step Six

Step Six – Confront Excuses/Resistance: Normal excuses can be dealt with by focusing the discussion on what people in the group can control. Keep the conversation forward looking and not focused on the past events that neither you nor the others can do anything about. Be firm; state your belief that something can be done and that with all of the intelligence in the meeting, something can be figured out. Don't let the meeting get sidetracked discussing excuses.

Some people play the role of a wet towel during a meeting. This is the person(s) who won't move forward, disagrees or argues with every point, doesn't contribute, or is disruptive. The meeting leader needs to bring this behavior out into the open and have it discussed by the group. Don't shy away from these people or attempt to ignore their behavior. Their actions are getting in the way of the meeting being effective. Surface what you see happening and discuss it in the group setting with the people involved; e.g., "We have been talking for an hour and no one has agreed to anything different. . .(silence)" or, "Every time we get close to a decision, Bob, you start talking about something else."

Step Seven – Clarify Consequences. Don't Punish: The conclusions or actions reached during the meeting represent an opportunity for the leader to reinforce and put into perspective the importance of carrying through with the plan. Be prepared to briefly summarize the benefits of implementing the actions, and ask the group for additional consequences. As in the coaching meeting, make your comments and the time spent on this step fit the situation. Don't overdo it.

Step Eight – Don't Give Up: The commitment and plan you documented on the flip chart serve as an excellent reference for future meetings. At these meetings, post the flip chart pages and review progress. Initiate problem-solving steps for those areas where the original actions are not meeting the objectives.

Many problems or opportunities discussed in a group are more complex than individual problems. The need for follow-up is even more critical since many smaller actions must be orchestrated to make for an overall success. We know of no situations where the first meeting was the last. Keep your meetings focused by starting with a review of the plans and accomplishments to date, and then discuss changes or additions that need to be made.

The Eight-Step Model can help you focus the attention of participants during future meetings, as well as improve the efficiency with which you work through agenda items. The use of a flip chart to document the thoughts leading up to and the conclusions for each of the 8 steps will also help your group stay on track and make the meeting more effective.

Step Seven

Step Eight

Keep your meetings focused

Appendix 1

THINKING IT THROUGH PLANNING GUIDE

1. Provide some background about the person you are coaching.

2. Describe how they or the situation is creating a concern. (Be specific, descriptive, and nonpunishing. What information do you have?)

3. What will ultimately happen if this person doesn't change/respond? (Is now the time to get heavy handed, or do you want to give the coaching process a chance to work?)

4. What immediate objective or initial solution do you want from the next coaching session? Let the employee be responsible for developing the means to reach the objective.

5. What is your overall long-range goal in working with this person?

6. Make a list of the reasons why it is to this person's advantage to change. Circle the three most important ones.

7. Describe your expectations and requirements for this person in terms of this immediate situation.

8. List statements that express three or four different forms of SUPPORT for this person.

9. How would you rate:
   a. your level of frustration with this issue?

   1_____10
   low   high

b. your exposure or the impact on you personally, if there is no change?

1_____10

low   high

c. the level of resistance and conflict that you have experienced in working with this employee?

1_____10

low   high

If you have two or more scores that are "6" or above, the chances of nonsupportive behavior, aggressiveness, and anger go up. You need to be cautious!

Are you able to devote 30 minutes or more, if necessary, to the coaching session?

(You run a risk of unfavorable results if you cannot allocate 30 minutes or more.)

Appendix 2

TRAINING DESIGN

"All leaders knew what to do. However, the best leaders applied it; the others did not."

Having read this far, you are probably saturated with information about the coaching process. More reading would fine tune your understanding, not build your proficiency. This comes only with practice. You have got to try it – not just once, but repeatedly.

There are two good reasons why managers are reluctant to try it.

1. Experimenting with the Eight-Step Model and the supporting skills may carry a higher risk than you're willing to assume. "It feels awkward. What if I don't do it right? How will the employees react? What if I make things worse? I don't have time. We're under too much pressure now to be experimenting." These are typical thoughts that keep managers from trying the concepts and skills.

2. There is no easy way to judge how you are doing and where improvements are needed. It's like trying to teach yourself how to play tennis – without feedback, you're guessing about what's being done right or wrong.

To overcome these obstacles, readers of this book may want to enroll in our Coaching Skills Seminar. The seminar provides an opportunity to:

- *participate in a risk-free learning environment that will help clarify the model*
- *receive feedback from professionals and peers on how you are doing and the impact of your behavior*

There is no more efficient way to start becoming the type of partner and coach described in this book than to attend our seminars, study and learn with others.

UNIQUENESS OF OUR COACHING SEMINAR

We teach the how to's of being an effective coach in a practical way by:

- *Exploring the subject in great depth.*
- *Using questionnaire feedback from team members.*
- *Allowing for flexibility in style.*
- *Offering post-seminar surveys to measure improvement.*
- *Using live demonstrations and video examples to illustrate the skills.*
- *Addressing the problem-solving, positive motivational, and creative coaching situations.*
- *Defining the specific supportive and initiative behaviors for effective coaching.*
- *Focusing on skill acquisition, practice, and feedback versus lecture and theory.*

PRE-SEMINAR WORK

Before the seminar, participants are asked to complete a questionnaire that assesses their coaching skills, as they see them. Participants also distribute similar questionnaires to their leaders, peers, and direct reports to get their perspective on the participant's coaching skills. These are mailed to the Center for Management and Organization Effectiveness for computer processing. The results are discussed during the seminar and action plans are prepared.

LEARNING FOUNDATIONS OF THE SEMINAR

1. Class discussion and practice versus lecture: 60% of the time is spent practicing the concepts and skills. The other 40% of the time is spent presenting the material and discussing questions. Formal lectures are kept to a minimum.
2. Practice sessions: Simulating a coaching session does four things:
   a. It allows a specific set of coaching behaviors to be highlighted and practiced.
   b. It allows participants to verbalize and express the skills in a very active yet risk-free way.
   c. It provides participants an opportunity to evaluate

their own strengths and weaknesses and to receive feedback from others.

d. It gives participants in depth practice on those skills or concepts they need to work on the most.

The practice sessions are conducted in a setting that is very supportive for the participants. We haven't discovered a better way to develop the participants' proficiencies than through realistic role plays.

Practice sessions are conducted in three-person teams. Each person rotates into the role of coach, team member, and observer during the session. The members of the groups are also changed throughout the seminar to provide variation and different perspectives for the participants.

3. Application planning: A final work-group session allows participants to practice the skills and concepts on an actual back home situation. This session will help start the transference of the skills learned.

THE SEMINAR

The sixteen-hour seminar can be conducted in any combination of four-hour time blocks. The following is the two-day agenda we use when conducting open, public enrollment workshops.

Day One

- *Introductions*
- *Seminar Objectives and Orientation*
- *Introduction to Coaching*
- *A Look at Your Coaching Style*
- *Introduction to the Coaching Model*
- *Lunch*
- *Analyzing Your Coaching Style*
- *Behavior Change Strategies*
- *Application of the Coaching Model*
- *Debriefing the Application/Case Study*
- *Questionnaire Feedback*
- *Review and Summary of the Day*

Day Two

- *Opening Remarks*
- *The Coaching Model, Steps One, Two, and Three*
- *Case Study*
- *The Coaching Model, Steps Four, Five, and Six*
- *Lunch*
- *Practice Exercise*
- *The Coaching Model, Steps Seven and Eight*
- *Small Group Practice*
- *Applying the Coaching Model Back on the Job*
- *Getting Started on Your Own Change*
- *Discussion, Questions, Seminar Evaluation*